# The
# WICKEDICTIONARY

Twisted definitions that perversely expose the truth

# Derek Abbott

2011 FALL

ISBN: 1463668260
ISBN-13: 9781463668266

# About the Author

Derek Abbott was born in South Kensington, London, UK, and is a well-known scientist. He regularly travels between the USA, the UK, and Australia as a speaker. He has previously lived in both the USA and the UK. He is married and presently lives in Adelaide, Australia.

His education began at Norland College pre-school, Chislehurst, Kent, UK, as a boarder and then he attended Oakfield School, Dulwich, UK, at the same time as the future singer Kim Wilde. His family moved to France, where he then attended the Ecole Seminaire de Collonges-sous-Salève (now Ecole Maurice-Tièche), France, and then the Ecole de Ferney-Voltaire (now Ecole Florian), France. On returning to the UK, he attended Bassett House School, London, UK and then boarded at Copthorne Preparatory School, Sussex, UK, at the same time as the future deputy editor of *Private Eye*, Francis Wheen. His family then moved to a Holland Park address where his neighbour was Gerry Conway, the drummer for Cat Stevens. His high school education took place at the infamous Holland Park School, London, UK, where the singer Yazz was one of his classmates. Here, he was taught English Literature by the comedian Mike Walling and music by Andy Mackay who later became the saxophonist of Roxy Music. He completed his bachelor's degree at Loughborough University of Technology, UK, and his PhD at the University of Adelaide, Australia.

**Dedicated to R**

# Table of Contents

# Introduction

The name *Wickedictionary* is intended to be a satirical play on the word *Wiktionary*. This is a collection of definitions of words as in a dictionary, except the definitions are perverse in the style of Ambrose Bierce's *The Devil's Dictionary*. For example:

> **Polygamy:** *n.* an act of supreme sacrifice where a man risks his life to more than one mother-in-law.

This is not a book of quotations, although the definitions are quotable. The idea is to modernize Ambrose Bierce, coming up with a more contemporary and cutting-edge collection of definitions. This is intended to be comical; there are no sides, and nothing is sacred here. Basically any definition that has a surprise twist qualifies for entry, whether it happens to be cynical or not. The idea is we don't have necessarily to agree with these definitions, but to merely enjoy them for making us think. As Aristotle once said, "It is the mark of an educated mind to be able to entertain a thought without accepting it."

# Acknowledgement

I'd like to thank my family for putting up with the birthing process for this book, which involved many hours wed to my computer. A special thanks goes to my mother who instilled in me, from an early age, a love of words and all forms of wordplay.

# An Invitation to the Reader

The reader is welcome to email the author anytime with suggestions at **wickedictionary@gmail.com** Personalized replies cannot be guaranteed due to the workload.

# Corrections

Each definition has a named author. If you notice any mistakes or can find a reference that identifies any definitions marked "Unknown" feel free to email me the details and source references.

Any definitions marked "Adapted from…" have altered the original wording to either fit into the dictionary format or modernize the language, with hopefully as little violence as possible to the original text. There are a few minor exceptions where some brutality was deemed appropriate, and the reader should not be overly alarmed or evacuate the planet on account of this.

# Reader Contributions

A number of definitions have already been contributed by readers, and further submissions are most welcome by emailing to the above address. You may make up your own twisted definitions or you can send me other existing ones with relevant citations to the literature.

Whilst this squalid collection is a haven for the cynic, the definitions do not have to be necessarily cynical in order to qualify for entry. We are not looking for play on words, but rather a perverted twist. Contradictory positions are encouraged, as no particular group, creed, or philosophy should escape a battering from every angle. The only rule is: if it makes me smile, I'll include it.

The reader may liken these definitions to a cartoonist's caricature of a face. The disproportionate facial features in a caricature are what amplify our ability to recognize the face and simultaneously lampoon the subject, all with deft efficiency. Likewise, some exaggeration in each definition is expected, as this is a legitimate literary device in order to draw attention to the truth.

Pleasantries and political correctness have no place here. Umberto Eco once suggested that war games and toy weapons enable children to work through repression and learn to understand consequences of violence in a safe space. The pen is mightier than the sword, and *The Wickedictionary* may be thought of as a safe adult play space where sacred cows are slaughtered for our edification. By sharpening our vision, in this way, we see the paradox of the human condition and are able to laugh at the stupidity of our species, in order for us move forward to make the world a better place. At the heart of every cynic, is a compassionate idealist bursting forth to save the universe.

# A

**Ability:** *n.* that which will never catch up with the demand for it.
**Confucius**

**Abstract art:** *n.* a product of the untalented, sold by the unprincipled to the utterly bewildered.
**Albert Camus**

**Absurdity:** *n.* a statement or belief manifestly inconsistent with one's own opinion.
**Ambrose Bierce**

**Academia:** *n.* a chronic disease characterized by a compulsion to write lengthy specialized treatises in unintelligible vocabularies, for the purpose of rising in the esteem of those similarly afflicted.
**Rick Bayan**

**Accordion:** *n.* a bagpipe with pleats.
**Unknown**

**Accountant:** *n.* 1. a dutiful book-balancer whose role within a corporation is to protect if from creative ideas.
**Rick Bayan**

**Accountant:** *n.* 2. a person who will prove that two and two did make four, but, after deduction of professional fees, now only comes to three.
**Unknown**

**Accusation:** *n.* a disguised confession, where the accuser projects his own misdemeanour upon a hapless bystander.
**Derek Abbott**

**Actor:** *n.* a professional exhibitionist who manufactures emotions in a manner convincing enough to earn a living.
**Rick Bayan**

**Addict:** *n.* a hobbyist with commitment.
**Contributed specially for *The Wickedictionary* by Julian O'Shea**

**Administration:** *n.* a virus that spreads throughout any organization that rapidly replicates to create more administration. Can be fatal.
**Derek Abbott**

**Admiration:** *n.* our feeling of delight that another person resembles us.
**Evan Esar**

**Adore:** *v.t.* to venerate expectantly.
**Ambrose Bierce**

**Adult:** *n.* 1. a person who has stopped growing at both ends and is now growing in the middle.
**Unknown**

**Adult:** *n.* 2. a socially obedient child.
**Contributed specially for *The Wickedictionary* by Jacob Irving**

**Adult:** *n.* 3. an obsolete child.
**Theodor Geisel (Dr. Suess)**

**Adultery:** *n.* 1. the application of democracy to love.
**H. L. Mencken**

**Adultery:** *n.* 2. the noble act of sharing taken to its logical limits.
**Derek Abbott**

**Adultery:** *n.* 3. an alarmingly popular sin that, despite its name, appeals primarily to those in search of a second adolescence.
**Rick Bayan**

**Advertising:** *n.* the rattling of a stick inside a swill-bucket.
**George Orwell**

**Afternoon:** *n.* that part of the day we spend worrying about how we wasted the morning.
**Unknown**

**Age:** *n.* the gift of acquiring eyesight too poor to notice any wrinkles.
**Contributed specially for *The Wickedictionary* by Cheryl Rae**

**Agent's fee:** *n.* the tribute that art pays to commerce.
**Rick Bayan**

**Agnostic:** *n.* one whose extreme skepticism even keeps them from being an atheist.
**Derek Abbott**

**Airport:** *n.* a destination to which we proceed with haste so that we can glance at our watches for the next two and a half hours.
**Rick Bayan**

**Air stewardess:** *n.* a mile-high waitress.
**Derek Abbott**

**Alcoholic:** *n.* someone you don't like who drinks as much as you do.
**Dylan Thomas**

**Alimony:** *n.* 1. is like buying hay for a dead horse.
**Grouch Marx**

**Alimony:** *n.* 2. the sum of money a man is commanded to pay his ex-wife in exchange for the pleasure of having her live under a separate roof.
**Rick Bayan**

**Alpha male:** *n.* a somewhat inferior specimen of the male species who excessively overcompensates for his lack of testosterone.
**Derek Abbott**

**Ambassador:** *n.* a wealthy person exiled to an alien land for the purpose of throwing parties, presumably with the hope of extracting government secrets from tipsy natives.
**Rick Bayan**

**Ambition:** *n.* 1. the last refuge of the failure.
**Oscar Wilde**

**Ambition:** *n.* 2. a poor excuse for not having enough sense to be lazy.
**Stephen Wright**

**Americans:** *n. pl.* escaped convicts, of which His Majesty is fortunate to be rid of such rabble.
**Oliver Sharpin**

**Amnesia:** *n.* a condition that enables a woman who has gone through labour to have sex again.
**Unknown**

**Amnesty:** *n.* the state's magnanimity to those offenders whom it would be too expensive to punish.
**Ambrose Bierce**

**Anarchist:** *n.* one who is disappointed with the future before it even happens.
**Unknown**

**Anger:** *n.* the feeling that makes your mouth work faster than your mind.
**Evan Esar**

**Anorexic:** *n.* exhibiting the alluring slimness of a skeleton, like the prose style of a minimalist writer.
**Rick Bayan**

**Antique:** *n.* an item your grandparents bought, your parents got rid of, and you're buying again.
**Unknown**

**Appeaser:** *n.* one who feeds a crocodile—hoping it will eat him last.
**Winston Churchill**

**Appeal:** *v.* (*legal term*) to put the dice in the box for another throw.
**Ambrose Bierce**

**A priori:** *adj.* the term applied to reasoning from pre-existing knowledge, or even cherished prejudices.
**The Chambers Dictionary, 1901**

**Assumption:** *n.* an error of which you are as yet unaware.
**Unknown**

**Aphorism:** *n.* pre-digested wisdom.
**Ambrose Bierce**

**Archbishop:** *n.* a Christian ecclesiastic of a rank superior to that attained by Christ.
**H. L. Mencken**

**Argument:** *n.* an exchange of words between people with diametrically opposed views, all of whom know that they are right.
**Unknown**

**Aristocracy:** *n.* another name for well-organized bad manners.
**Unknown**

**Art:** *n.* 1. moral passion married to entertainment. Moral passion without entertainment is propaganda, and entertainment without moral passion is television.
**Rita Mae Brown**

**Art:** *n.* 2. a step from what is obvious and well-known toward what is arcane and concealed.
**Khalil Gibran**

**Art:** *n.* 3. a collaboration between God and the artist, and the less the artist does the better.
**André Gide**

**Art:** *n.* 4. magic delivered from the lie of being truth.
**Theodor Adorno**

**Artificial insemination:** *n.* procreation without recreation.
**Rick Bayan**

**Artist:** *n.* 1. somebody who produces things that people don't need to have.
**Andy Warhol**

**Artist:** *n.* 2. being an artist means ceasing to take seriously that very serious person we are when we are not an artist.
**Jose Ortega y Gasset**

**Artist:** *n.* 3. a questing soul who pursues a singular vision, creates something of permanent value, and dies with the rent unpaid.
**Rick Bayan**

**Assassination:** *n.* the extreme form of censorship.
**George Bernard Shaw**

**Assonance:** *n.* a rhyme that has gone wrong.
**Adapted from Willy Russell's play *Educating Rita***

**Astrologer:** *n.* an otherwise jobless New Age savant who has convinced his clientele that his ability to foretell the distant future is measurably more reliable that his recall of past events from last night's 6 o'clock news.
**Derek Abbott**

**Astrology:** *n.* an ancient pseudoscience and barroom conversation starter founded on the premise that everyone born under the same stars will meet a dark

stranger, receive a propitious business offer, or suffer an attack of dyspepsia on the same day.
**Rick Bayan**

**Atheism:** *n.* 1. one's God-given right to not believe.
**Derek Abbott**

**Atheism:** *n.* 2. a godless religion that retains all the dogmatic posturing of the faiths it so confidently denies, with few of the consolations.
**Rick Bayan**

**Atheist:** *n.* 1. the ultimate gambler.
**Unknown**

**Atheist:** *n.* 2. someone who's all dressed up with no place to go after death.
**Adapted from James Duffecy**

**Atheist:** *n.* 3. one who requires an indefinitely greater measure of faith than to receive all the great truths which atheism would deny.
**Joseph Addison**

**Atheist:** *n.* 4. one with blind faith in a mistaken belief that the absence of evidence against a null hypothesis confirms it.
**Derek Abbott**

**Atheist:** *n.* 5. a person who believes in one less god than you do.
**Donald Morgan**

**Atheist:** *n.* 6. a man who believes himself to be an accident.
**Francis Thompson**

**Atheist:** *n.* 7. a person who dines at a lavish banquet, believing there is no kitchen, no waste chute, nor chef.
**Derek Abbott**

**Atheist:** *n.* 8. God's loyal opposition.
**Woody Allen**

**Attraction:** *n.* a special ingredient that, if missing, transforms 'hot date' into 'stalker'.
**Derek Abbott**

**Australia:** *n.* a country lying in the South Sea, whose industrial and commercial development has been unspeakably retarded by an unfortunate dispute among geographers as to whether it is a continent or an island.
**Ambrose Bierce**

**Author:** *n.* a writer with connections in the publishing industry.
**Rick Bayan**

**Autobiography:** *n.* a book written about oneself, now often written by somebody else.
***Chambers Gigglossary***

# B

**Bachelor:** *n.* one who knows more about women than married men; if they didn't they'd be married too.
**H. L. Mencken**

**Backlash:** *n.* the equal and opposite reaction to actions on behalf of women, minorities, political correctness, jogging, spotted owls, oat bran and other timely causes, sometimes legitimate, that have been marketed to the public with fatally obnoxious zeal.
**Unknown**

**Bagpipes:** *n.* an instrument of torture used by the Scots against other nations.
*Chambers Gigglossary*

**Bail:** *n.* an opportunity to see if you can get away with it the second time.
*Chambers Gigglossary*

**Bank:** *n.* 1. a place where money automatically increases in value, especially when we need to borrow some.
**Rick Bayan**

**Bank:** *n.* 2. an institution that lends money that doesn't actually exist.
**Derek Abbott**

**Banker:** *n.* one who lends you his umbrella when the sun is shining, but wants it back the minute it begins to rain.
**Attributed to Mark Twain**

**Banking:** *n.* a form of legalized theft where vast profits are made on transactions of monetary instruments that are not underpinned by true products and services, leading to rather spectacular global market crashes from time to time. *See Pyramid scheme.*
**Derek Abbott**

**Bargain:** *n.* something you can't use offered at a price you can't resist.
*Chambers Gigglossary*

**Baritone:** *n.* (*operatic term*) unlike a tenor, a baritone is one who always sings about himself.
*The Ten Tenors*

**Bartender:** *n.* a pharmacist with a limited inventory.
**Unknown**

**Bathroom:** *n.* a room used by the entire family, believed by all except mothers to be self-cleaning.
**Unknown**

**Belladonna:** *n.* in Italian a beautiful lady; in English a deadly poison. A striking example of the essential identity of the two tongues.
**Ambrose Bierce**

**Belt:** *n.* worn around the waist to give other people the impression that one is slim enough to require it.
**Unknown**

**Big bang:** *n.* the primordial slap on the backside of the newborn universe.
**Rick Bayan**

**Bigotry:** *n.* that which tries to keep truth safe in a grip so tight that it kills it.
**Adapted from Rabindranath Tagore**

**Bimbo:** *n.* one whose IQ is smaller than their bra size.
**Contributed specially for *The Wickedictionary* by Rach Shagwell**

**Biography:** *n.* a system in which the contradictions of a human life are unified.
**Jose Ortega y Gasset**

**Birthday:** *n.* the unique celebration of being one Earth's orbit closer to death.
**Contributed specially for *The Wickedictionary* by Julian O'Shea**

**Black holes:** *n.* are where God divided by zero.
**Steven Wright**

**Blogs:** *n.* proof that infinite monkeys on infinite typewriters will only produce grammatically incorrect, self-indulgent ramblings.
**Contributed specially for *The Wickedictionary* by Julian O'Shea**

**Bonus:** *n.* money your boss gets each year for controlling your department's costs. Of course, if he paid your bonus he wouldn't achieve that target.
**Isham Research**

**Bookcase:** *n.* a piece of furniture used in America to house bowling trophies and Elvis collectibles.
**Rick Bayan**

**Bore:** *n.* 1. a person who talks when you wish him to listen.
**Ambrose Bierce**

**Bore:** *n.* 2. a man who deprives you of solitude without providing you with company.
**Gian Vincenzo Gravina**

**Bore:** *n.* 3. a man who, when you ask him how he is, tells you.
**Bert Leston Taylor**

**Bore:** *n.* 4. one who leaves nothing out.
**Adapted from Voltaire**

**Boss:** *n.* 1. someone who is early when you are late and late when you are early.
**Unknown**

**Boss:** *n.* 2. a personal dictator appointed to those of us fortunate enough to live in free societies.
**Rick Bayan**

**Bravery:** *n.* a dizzying combination of luck and stupidity; the act of one who miscalculates the risks and yet survives by pure chance.
**Derek Abbott**

**Brevity:** *n.* the soul of lingerie.
**Dorothy Parker**

**Bribe:** *n.* a tip in advance.
**Derek Abbott**

**Bride:** *n.* a woman with a fine prospect of happiness behind her.
**Ambrose Bierce**

**Broadsheet newspaper:** *n.* a device for helping fools to feel superior.
**Contributed specially for *The Wickedictionary* by Joshua Arnold-Foster**

**Building regulations:** *n.* local civic laws regulating the construction of buildings, devised to make planning a bungalow in the twentieth century slower than building a cathedral in the twelfth century.
**Adapted from Jonathan Lynn and Anthony Jay**

**Bureaucracy:** *n.* 1. an ingenious scheme by benevolent governments for graciously providing unlimited mass employment.
**Derek Abbott**

**Bureaucracy:** *n.* 2. a group of overeducated and underwhelming individuals who combine mystification and ineffectiveness in order to facilitate entropy.
**Contributed specially for** *The Wickedictionary* **by David Olney**

**Bureaucracy:** *n.* 3. a government-funded distortion of national unemployment figures.
**Contributed specially for** *The Wickedictionary* **by Karen Rossiter**

**Bureaucracy:** *n.* 4. a stubborn clog in the sewer pipe of government.
**Rick Bayan**

**Business:** *n.* organized cheating.
**Leonard Rossiter**

# C

**Canada:** *n.* according to the U.S., a land that will never be great so long as it continues to burden its citizens with universal health care, refuses to drill for oil in federally protected wildlife reserves, and neglects its duty to blindly support unilateral invasions of Middle Eastern states.
**Adapted from *The Onion***

**Car:** *n.* a motorized cubicle on wheels in which holding a phone whilst driving is illegal. However, shaving, knitting, origami folding, eating, undressing, and performing lewd acts whilst driving are perfectly acceptable and fundamental to human liberty.
**Derek Abbott**

**Capitalism:** *n.* survival of the fattest.
**Unknown**

**Capital punishment:** *n.* the controversial right of the state to end a life by gassing, shooting, hanging, needling or quick-frying; believed effective as a deterrent to future crimes by the same individual.
**Rick Bayan**

**Catholic clergy:** *n.* God's stormtroopers.
**Dave Allen**

**Catholicism:** *n.* a powerful multilateral platform working under the ill-informed belief of its own righteousness. Noted for use of effective group think methodologies spanning from the 11th century to the 19th century in order to sustain power and control. *See Inquisition.*
**Contributed specially for *The Wickedictionary* by K**

**Canonization:** *n.* a posthumous elevation to sainthood; a state of grace attained by religious leaders through miracles, by politicians via assassination, and by rock stars as a result of a timely drug overdose.
**Rick Bayan**

**CD player:** *n.* an irritating toy that restores life to dead noises.
**Adapted from Leonard Rossiter**

**Celebrity:** *n.* someone who is known to many persons he is glad he doesn't know.
**H. L. Mencken**

**Celibacy:** *n.* 1. a renouncement of pleasures of the flesh followed by indefinite abstinence, usually lasting no more than three days with best of intentions.
**Derek Abbott**

**Celibacy:** *n.* 2. a respite from the pleasures and perils of sexual congress; a way of life traditionally practiced by Catholic priests, monks, Shakers, stamp collectors, overly zealous careerists, Star Trek fans, hermits, and amoebas.
**Rick Bayan**

**Celibacy:** *n.* 3. mind over hormones.
**Derek Abbott**

**Censor:** *n.* a man who knows more than he thinks you ought to.
**Granville Hicks**

**Chess:** *n.* a foolish expedient for making idle people believe they are doing something very clever, when they are only wasting their time.
**George Bernard Shaw**

**Chicken:** *n.* an animal you eat before it's born and after it's dead.
**Unknown**

**Chihuahua:** *n.* a Mexican rat, which is sometimes mistaken for a dog.
**Unknown**

**Childhood:** *n.* the rapidly shrinking interval between infancy and first arrest on a drug or weapons charge.
**Rick Bayan**

**Cinnamon:** *n.* sawdust.
**Derek Abbott**

**City:** *n.* a community that has grown sufficiently in size that there is rather more than just one village idiot.
**Derek Abbott**

**Civilization:** *n.* the limitless multiplication of unnecessary necessities.
**Mark Twain**

**Classic:** *n.* a book that everyone praises, but no one reads.
**Adapted from Mark Twain**

**Clergyman:** *n.* the official custodian of a religious congregation's ancient tribal beliefs, appointed so that members can leave spiritual matters to a qualified professional while they go about the business of sinning and making a living.
**Rick Bayan**

**Closet homosexual:** *n.* a man who's yet to get in touch with his inner bitch.
**Contributed specially for *The Wickedictionary* by Rach Shagwell**

**Clothing:** *n.* a means to allow nakedness at one's choosing.
**Derek Abbott**

**Cocktail party:** *n.* a device for paying off obligations to people you don't want to invite to dinner.
**Charles Merrill Smith**

**Coincidence:** *n.* a powerful aphrodisiac.
**Contributed specially for *The Wickedictionary* by John Ruffels**

**College:** *n.* the four-year period when parents are permitted access to the telephone.
**Unknown**

**Colloquialism:** *n.* a formal word for an informal word.
**David Cook**

**Comedian:** *n.* one whose duty it is to find out where the line is drawn and cross it deliberately.
**Adapted from George Carlin**

**Comedy:** *n.* is simply a funny way of being serious.
**Peter Ustinov**

**Commitment:** *n.* the capacity of a would-be husband to do what he's told.
**Warren Keyes**

**Committee:** *n.* 1. individuals who can do nothing individually and sit and decide that nothing can be done together.
**Unknown**

**Committee:** *n.* 2. a group of the unwilling, picked from the unfit, to do the unnecessary.
**Richard Harkness**

**Committee:** *n.* 3. a cul-de-sac down which ideas are lured and then quietly strangled.
**Sir Barnett Cock**

**Communism:** *n.* 1. is largely made up of prophecies, like any other revealed religion.
**Adapted from H. L. Mencken**

**Communism:** *n.* 2. liberation of the people from the burdens of liberty.
**Rick Bayan**

**Communist:** *n.* in the UK, a child of the 1950s with hippy tendencies who fought for unionism, despised bourgeois values, and lived in the poorest regions of London's East End. These formerly squalid living quarters are now trendy upwardly mobile lodgings, reaping the benefits of successive property price booms, transforming their eager owners into well-coiffed landlords with all the values they once spurned.
**Derek Abbott**

**Common sense:** *n.* is nothing more than a deposit of prejudices laid down by the mind before you reach eighteen.
**Albert Einstein**

**Compiler:** *n.* (*computing term*) a program written specifically to treat a higher level language program as data, reduce some of it to machine code, rearrange the rest into another higher level language such as Greek, display an alarming and incomprehensible message such as 'Fatal Internal Stack Failure' and then give up.
**John Norris**

**Comprehensive school:** *n.* in the UK, a large-scale plant for the systematic production of consistent mediocrity.
**Leonard Rossiter**

**Comprehensive school:** *n.* in the UK, an educational abortion, a vast factory, mass-producing units for the prefabrication of the classless dictatorship of the proletariat.
**Unknown**

**Compromise:** *n.* the art of dividing a cake in such a way that everyone believes he got the bigger piece.
**Unknown**

**Computer:** *n.* 1. an electronic time-saving device that is commonly used for time-wasting activities.
**Warwick Annear**

**Computer:** *n.* 2. a modern device for spewing out great quantities of scrap paper and incorrect information.
**Leonard Rossiter**

**Computer virus:** *n.* a welcomed device for keeping anti-virus software manufacturers in business.
**Derek Abbott**

**Concept:** *n.* any idea for which an outside consultant billed you more than $25,000.
**Unknown**

**Conception:** *n.* the miracle of producing losers from winners.
**Contributed specially for** *The Wickedictionary* **by Lloyd Irving**

**Conclusion:** *n.* the place where you got tired of thinking.
**Stephen Wright**

**Conference:** *n.* the confusion of one person multiplied by the number present.
**Unknown**

**Conference room:** *n.* a place where everyone talks, no one listens, and everyone disagrees later.
**Unknown**

**Confession:** *n.* a declaration of one's faults. Often done by confessing little faults, to suggest the absence of big ones.
**Unknown**

**Confidence:** *n.* the feeling one experiences before one fully understands the situation.
***Chambers Gigglossary***

**Confidential:** *n.* won't be leaked to the newspapers until later today.
**Adapted from Jonathan Lynn and Anthony Jay**

**Conflict of interest:** *n.* 1. an ingenious mechanism for reluctantly forfeiting time consuming professional duties, avoiding committee meetings, and dodging jury service.
**Derek Abbott**

**Conflict of interest:** *n.* 2. in the US, the reason cited why government officials are not allowed to let you pay their lunch bill, thereby implying they are so cheap that they can be bribed with only one business lunch.
**Derek Abbott**

**Conflict of interest:** *n.* 3. in the US, the reason for impeaching a president if he has inappropriate relations with a junior staff member, but is perfectly acceptable when generously handing out post-war reconstruction contracts to all your buddies.
**Derek Abbott**

**Conflict of interest:** *n.* 4. an ethical principle that precludes one inappropriately taking part in an activity, but unfortunately does not count as a reason to exclude you from wartime army service.
**Derek Abbott**

**Conflict of interest:** *n.* 5. what is automatically suspected if you don't declare it, but is unquestioned if you declare it and eagerly leave a committee meeting.
**Derek Abbott**

**Conflict of interest:** *n.* 6. the situation that occurs when a government punishes the people for its dependence on discredited substances (e.g., tobacco, carbon, etc.) by raising taxes on them, thereby increasing the government's own dependence.
**Derek Abbott**

**Congratulation:** *n.* the civility of envy.
**Ambrose Bierce**

**Conscience:** *n.* 1. the inner voice that warns us somebody may be looking.
**H. L. Mencken**

**Conscience:** *n.* 2. that which hurts when all your other parts feel so good.
**Unknown**

**Conscience:** *n.* 3. Is what makes a boy tell his mother before his sister does.
**Evan Esar**

**Conscience:** *n.* 4. that which makes cowards of us all.
**Adapted from Shakespeare**

**Conscience:** *n.* 5. an anticipation of other people's opinions.
**Unknown**

**Conservative:** *n.* 1. one who admires radicals centuries after they're dead.
**Leo Rosten**

**Conservative:** *n.* 2. a statesman who is enamored of existing evils, as distinguished from the Liberal who wishes to replace them with others.
**Ambrose Bierce**

**Conservative:** *n.* 3. in the US, one who believes that non-conservatives in other countries are either 'commies' or socialists and that conservatives in other countries are either despots or terrorists.
**Derek Abbott**

**Conservative:** *n.* 4. one tending to maintain existing views and conditions; often extending to faithfully conserving his maturity from when he was nine years old.
**Derek Abbott**

**Conservative:** *n.* 5. in the US, one with a faith so large that he can move mountains, dispel global warming, and cause abiotic oil to eternally spout forth from the earth.
**Derek Abbott**

**Conservative:** *n.* 6. in the U.S., a decent fellow who counsels the poor to earn pennies for their daily bread, while he and his family dine nightly on filet mignon.
**Rick Bayan**

**Conservative:** *n.* 7. one who adopts old worn out views once invented by radicals.
**Adapted from Mark Twain**

**Conservative**: *n.* 8. one who'd give anything to stamp out pacifism and other liberal evils in his own country, and yet ironically prays for enemy nations to vote for peace-loving liberal governments.
**Derek Abbott**

**Conservative:** *n.* 9. in the US, one who rejects the control of big government, but willingly submits to the dictatorship of big corporations.
**Derek Abbott**

**Conservative**: *n.* 10. in the US, one who idolizes the virtues of Darwinism in all spheres of life from economics to national defence, yet vigorously denies its existence in biology.
**Derek Abbott**

**Conservative:** *n.* 11. in the US, one who doesn't accept climate science and doesn't even want the word French in French fries, yet waxes lyrical about French nuclear power that reduces French emissions.
**Adapted from Jeffrey Kluger**

**Conservative**: *n.* 12. in the US, one who believes big government always messes up the country on domestic policy, yet is miraculously blameless on matters of foreign policy.
**Derek Abbott**

**Conservative**: *n.* 13. in the US, one who believes in trickle down economics, but forgets it's only a trickle.
**Derek Abbott**

**Consistent:** *n.* dead.
**Adapted from Aldous Huxley**

**Consistency:** *n.* 1. the last refuge of the unimaginative.
**Oscar Wild**

**Consistency:** *n.* 2. the enemy of enterprise, just as symmetry is the enemy of art.
**George Bernard Shaw**

**Conspiracy theory:** *n.* the selective use of Occam's razor that joins up all the factual dots in the simplest way, but at the expense of assuming a rather complicated set of underlying motives put into action by flawless forward planning.
**Derek Abbott**

**Consult:** *v.* to seek approval for a course of action already decided upon.
**Ambrose Bierce**

**Consultant:** *n.* 1. a jobless person who shows executives how to work.
**Rick Bayan**

**Consultant:** *n.* 2. one who has credibility because he's not dumb enough to work at your company.
**Adapted from Scott Adams**

**Consultant:** *n.* 3. a person who is called in when no one wants to take the blame for what is going on.
**Unknown**

**Contraception:** *n.* an opportunity for one party to 'accidentally' produce a pregnancy without mutual consent.
**Derek Abbott**

**Contract:** *n.* a document that makes extortion legal.
*Chambers Gigglossary*

**Cordon bleu:** *n.* a term used to describe an individual who is particularly adept at disguising food.
**Leonard Rossiter**

**Correctional facility:** *n.* rent-free public housing for thieves, rapists, muggers, murderers, deadbeats, extortionists, drug fiends, and other assorted malcontents who are thought to benefit from confinement in each other's company.
**Rick Bayan**

**Corruption:** *n.* nature's way of restoring our faith in democracy.
**Peter Ustinov**

**Corporation:** *n.* 1. an ingenious device for obtaining individual profit without individual responsibility.
**Ambrose Bierce**

**Corporation:** *n.* 2. a miniature totalitarian state governed by a hierarchy of unelected officials who take a dim view of individualism, free speech, equality, and eggheads.
**Rick Bayan**

**Cosmetics:** *n.* 1. a means of presenting goods without necessarily guaranteeing their delivery.
**Contributed specially for *The Wickedictionary* by Lloyd Irving**

**Cosmetics:** *n.* 2. an arsenal of facial enhancements commonly applied in excess by women and male celebrities who feel the need to look embalmed.
**Rick Bayan**

**Cosmetics:** *n.* 3. used for enhancing a woman's beauty—a sign of things not necessarily to come.
**Contributed specially for *The Wickedictionary* by Cheryl Rae**

**Cosmetologist:** *n.* one who studies black holes in the skin, as opposed to a cosmologist, who studies them in the universe.
**Contributed specially for *The Wickedictionary* by Jessica Drouin**

**Country:** *n.* a piece of land with an imaginary border, across which the flow of travellers is forcibly controlled. A device that bestows a basic freedom to migrating birds, but denies the same to humans.
**Derek Abbott**

**Courage:** *n.* is often lack of insight, whereas cowardice in many cases is based on good information.
**Peter Ustinov**

**Courtesy:** *n.* 1. the art of yawning with your mouth closed.
**Unknown**

**Courtesy:** *n.* 2. a form of polite behaviour practiced by civilized people when they have time.
**Unknown**

**Cover up:** *n.* responsible discretion exercised in the national interest to prevent unnecessary disclosure of eminently justifiable procedures in which an untimely revelation would severely impair public confidence.
**Jonathan Lynn and Anthony Jay**

**Creativity:** *n.* 1. is knowing how to hide your sources.
**Albert Einstein**

**Creativity:** *n.* 2. is allowing yourself to make mistakes. Art is knowing which ones to keep.
**Scott Adams**

**Credit:** *n.* (*finance term*) a gift that keeps on taking.
**Unknown**

**Criminal:** *n.* a person with predatory instincts who hasn't sufficient capital to form a corporation.
**Unknown**

**Criminal lawyer:** *n.* a tautology.
**Unknown**

**Critic:** *n.* one who searches for ages for the wrong word, which, to give due credit, is eventually found.
**Adapted from Peter Ustinov**

**Criticism:** *n.* is prejudice made plausible.
**H. L. Mencken**

**Crouton:** *n.* stale bread.
**Adapted from George Carlin**

**Cuba:** *n.* an island that has perfected Communism, creating a truly equal society where desperate poverty is distributed evenly among all citizens.
**Adapted from *The Onion***

**Cubicle:** *n.* a sensory deprivation chamber designed to boost productivity in the workplace, at least according to people who work in corner offices with large windows.
**Rick Bayan**

**Cubism:** *n.* is where the laws of perspective have been repealed.
**Adapted from Bill Watterson's *Calvin & Hobbes***

**Cuddling:** *n.* a sweetly chaste form of intimacy that tends to make the average man feel like a muzzled hound on a foxhunt.
**Rick Bayan**

**Cult film:** *n.* a movie seen about fifty times by about that many people.
**Rick Bayan**

**Cynic:** *n.* 1. a man who, when he smells flowers, looks around for a coffin.
**Attributed to H. L. Mencken**

**Cynic:** *n.* 2. is what an idealist calls a realist.
**Jonathan Lynn and Anthony Jay**

**Cynic:** *n.* 3. a man who knows the price of everything and the value of nothing.
**Oscar Wilde**

**Cynic:** *n.* 4. an idealist whose rose-coloured glasses have been removed, snapped in two, and stomped into the ground, immediately improving his vision.
**Rick Bayan**

**Cynic:** *n.* 5. a person searching for an honest man, with a stolen lantern.
**Edgar A. Shoaff**

**Cynic:** *n.* 6. a blackguard whose faulty vision sees things as they are, not as they ought to be.
**Ambrose Bierce**

**Cynic:** *n.* 7. one who is prematurely disappointed in the future.
**Sidney J. Harris**

**Cynicism:** *n.* the fine art of expressing the truth without its pants on.
**Derek Abbott**

# D

**Dancing:** *n.* a perpendicular expression of a horizontal desire.
**George Bernard Shaw**

**Danger:** *n.* a perilous situation that arises if you are right in matters on which the established authorities are wrong.
**Adapted from Voltaire**

**Date:** *n.* an opportunity to find out why another person is still single.
**Unknown**

**Dating:** *v.t.* an elaborate prelude to mating that fulfils much the same function as the sniffing ritual in dogs, but without its forthright honesty.
**Rick Bayan**

**Die:** *v.* to stop sinning suddenly.
**Elbert Hubbard**

**Death:** *n.* 1. that which is caused by swallowing small amounts of saliva over a long period of time.
**George Carlin**

**Death:** *n.* 2. a fascinating journey where you get to touch a new dimension, but where you ain't coming back.

**Contributed specially for *The Wickedictionary* by Lochy Cupitt**

**Debugging:** *n.* (*computing term*) the process of removing software bugs, as opposed to programming that is the process of putting them in.

**Adapted from Edsger Dijkstra**

**Decisive:** *adj.* a person who is decisive is one who does not have the patience to carefully study all the possibilities.

**Derek Abbott**

**Defence:** *n.* an illusion of security for the public, not the enemy.

**Adapted from Jonathan Lynn and Anthony Jay**

**Definition:** *n.* the act of legislating meanings through clever word play.

**Karim Murji**

**Democratic election:** *n.* a pork barrel load of promises.

**Derek Abbott**

**Democratic party:** *n.* an organization with contradictory policies designed to appeal to the middle ground for attracting marginal voters.

**Contributed specially for *The Wickedictionary* by Reginald P. Coutts**

**Democracy:** *n.* 1. the theory that the common people know what they want, and deserve to get it good and hard.
**H. L. Menken**

**Democracy:** *n.* 2. is a form of worship; it is the worship of jackals by jackasses.
**Attributed to H. L. Mencken**

**Democracy:** *n.* 3. the pathetic belief in the wisdom of collective ignorance.
**Attributed to H. L. Mencken**

**Democracy:** *n.* 4. a place where numerous elections are held at great cost without issues and with interchangeable candidates.
**Gore Vidal**

**Democracy:** *n.* 5. the recurrent suspicion that more than half of the people are right more than half of the time.
**E. B. White**

**Democracy:** *n.* 6. true democracy is that one moron is equal to one genius.
**Leo Szilard**

**Democracy:** *n.* 7. a democracy is the name politicians give to their electorate when they need them.
**Unknown**

**Democracy:** *n.* 8. a system which ensures that everybody gets what nobody wants.
**Iain Leonard**

**Democracy:** *n.* 9. a dictatorship by the corporations with the money to influence mindless votes.
**Derek Abbott**

**Democracy:** *n.* 10. that which guarantees an equality of opportunity, but not an equality of conditions.
**Adapted from Irving Kristol**

**Democracy:** *n.* 11. a system whereby uncertainty is used to select a government, as the process is driven by indecisive swing voters.
**Derek Abbott**

**Denial:** *n.* that which keeps an optimist from becoming a pessimist.
**Rick Bayan**

**Depression:** *n.* 1. that which causes women to either eat or go shopping, or men to invade another country.
**Adapted from Elayne Boosler**

**Depression:** *n.* 2. one-sided bipolar disorder.
**Derek Abbott**

**Desk:** *n.* a semi-mythical structure believed to exist underneath all your paperwork.
**Unknown**

**Dictator:** *n.* the alpha male in a tribe of baboons.
**Rick Bayan**

**Diplomacy:** *n.* the patriotic art of lying for one's country.
**Ambrose Bierce**

**Diplomat:** *n.* a person who can tell you to go to hell in such a way that you actually look forward to the trip.
**Caskie Stinnett**

**Disciplinarian:** *n.* one who selflessly improves the performance of others by dangling the threat of punishment over them for their rightful edification.
**Derek Abbott**

**Discontentment:** *n.* an absurdly exaggerated idea of the happiness of others.
**Unknown**

**Discretion:** *n.* secrecy.
**Jonathan Lynn and Anthony Jay**

**Disk crash:** *n.* a typical computer response to any critical deadline.
**Unknown**

**Divorce:** *n.* 1. the one human tragedy that reduces everything to cash.
**Rita Mae Brown**

**Divorce:** *n.* 2. from the Latin word meaning to rip out a man's genitals through his wallet.
**Robin Williams**

**Divorce:** *n.* 3. the future tense of marriage.
**Unknown**

**Dressed:** *n.* the state of being naked under one's clothing.
**Derek Abbott**

**Doctor:** *n.* the same as a lawyer; the only difference is that lawyers merely rob you, whereas doctors rob you and kill you too.
**Anton Chekhov**

**Dogmatic:** *adj.* a characteristic of those too afraid to admit a cat's whisker of doubt.
**Derek Abbott**

**Do-gooder:** *n.* one with no time to be good, as he is too busy doing good.
**Adapted from Rabindranath Tagore**

**Dog owners:** *n. pl.* cowards who haven't got the guts to bite people themselves.
**August Strindberg**

**Dot-com:** *n.* a valiant online enterprise that typically favors coolness over profitability; for this reason, esp.

following the Crash of 2000, now commonly referred to by traumatized investors as a 'dotbomb.'
**Rick Bayan**

**Doubt:** *n.* 1. is a pain too lonely to know that faith is his twin brother.
**Kahlil Gibran**

**Doubt:** *n.* 2. that which grows with knowledge.
**Johann Wolfgang von Goethe**

**Doubt:** *n.* 3. an absolute certainty in the belief that nothing is black and white.
**Derek Abbott**

**Doubt:** *n.* 4. beliefs are what divide people. Doubt unites them.
**Peter Ustinov**

**Downsizing:** *v.* the act of ejecting a large number of employees from a company; as opposed to firing, a term reserved for the privileged few.
**Derek Abbott**

**Drugs:** *n. pl.* in the 1960s, were substances like LSD that made the world look weird, now it's ones like Prozac to make the world look normal.
**Unknown**

**Dumped** *n.* the state in which your latest love interest has selflessly relieved you of any obligation to put up with a lifetime of their toxic behaviour. There are three types of dump: (i) the honest dump is when you are told you are incompatible on the first date. This in fact saves you of a lifetime of misery and is the most sought-after variety; (ii) the dishonest dump is when you are strung along dating for many years, nagged to spend a fortune on diamonds, and then dumped; (iii) the psycho dump is when you are dumped in hell-fire anger on the second date after a minor infraction, such as inconsiderately forgetting to phone that same night to soothe their insecurities. The psycho dumper is one whose honesty of emotion finally wins over their dishonesty of mind, at least releasing you from a life of eternal torment.

**Derek Abbott**

**Dust:** *n.* mud with all the juice sucked out.
**Unknown**

**Dyslexia:** *n.* a medical condition whose sufferers couldn't possibly spell it.
**Nigel Drury**

# E

**Eat:** *v.* to appropriate by destruction.
**Jean-Paul Sartre**

**Eclair:** *n.* a cake, long in shape but short in duration.
**Chambers Dictionary, 1952**

**Economic growth:** *n.* paying out twice as much in taxes as one formerly got in wages.
**Adapted from H. L. Mencken**

**Economic sanctions:** *n.* a welcomed ticket for a dictator to stir up internal patriotism that gives him *carte blanche* to exert an even tighter stranglehold on his regime.
**Derek Abbott**

**Economist:** *n.* an expert who will know tomorrow why the things he predicted yesterday didn't happen today.
**Laurence J. Peter**

**Economy:** *n.* a complex system of bankruptcies, loans, and overdrafts.
**Adapted from Leonard Rossiter**

**Edgy:** *n.* sufficiently abrasive and obnoxious to captivate an urban audience.
**Rick Bayan**

**Editor:** *n.* in the publishing industry, a diligent intellectual drudge condemned to a lifetime of embarrassingly meagre pay, so that multi-thousand-dollar contracts might be awarded to semi-literate celebrities for their ghost-written memoirs.
**Rick Bayan**

**Education:** *n.* 1. the thing that interferes with learning.
**Albert Einstein**

**Education:** *n.* 2. a method whereby one acquires a higher grade of prejudices.
**Laurence J. Peter**

**Egoist:** *n.* 1. person of low taste, more interested in himself than in me.
**Ambrose Bierce**

**Egoist:** *n.* 2. one who rises above the slimy obsequiousness that humility brings.
**Derek Abbott**

**Egotism:** *n.* the anesthetic given by a kindly nature to relieve the pain of being a damned fool.
**Bellamy Brooks**

**Elder:** *n.* one who asserts his authority over you by virtue of his immutable age difference, but to whose chagrin finds that you rapidly sneak up to him in terms of age ratio.
**Derek Abbott**

**Election:** *n.* 1. a democratic ritual carried out in order to check if the polls were right.
**Derek Abbott**

**Election:** *n.* 2. that in which each party steals so many articles of faith from the other, and the candidates spend so much time making each other's speeches, that by the time election day is past there is nothing much to do save turn the sitting rascals out and let a new gang in.
**H. L. Mencken**

**Election:** *n.* 3. a sort of advance auction sale of stolen goods.
**H. L. Mencken**

**Electricity:** *n.* is really just organized lightning.
**George Carlin**

**Electrocution:** *n.* burning at the stake with all the modern improvements.
**Unknown**

**Emissions trading:** *n.* 1. a brilliant mechanism allowing corporations to pollute the environment guilt-free, whilst driving up the prices for further corporate gain.
**Derek Abbott**

**Emissions trading:** *n.* 2. a pollution control scheme that is rather like allowing a criminal to buy his way out of jail based on finding one honest person in the world to apparently reduce the overall crime footprint.
**Derek Abbott**

**Employee:** *n.* one who has sold both his body and soul to the corporation, as opposed to a prostitute whose body is only on hire for short intervals.
**Derek Abbott**

**Encryption:** *n.* (*computing term*) a powerful algorithmic encoding technique designed to deny useful content to casual readers. Often used in the creation of computer manuals.
**Isham Research**

**Enemy:** *n.* 1. (*foreign policy term*) a fiction abroad to distract us from domestic reality.
**Derek Abbott**

**Enemy:** *n.* 2. anyone who tells the truth about you.
**Elbert Hubbard**

**Enemy:** *n.* 3. a friend who you got to know better.
**Unknown**

**Enemy:** *n.* 4. one who backstabs you, as opposed to a true friend who stabs you in the front.
**Adapted from Oscar Wilde**

**English:** *n.* the English are those with the most rigid code of immorality in the world.
**Adapted from Malcolm Bradbury**

**Englishman:** *n.* one who instinctively admires any man who has no talent and is modest about it.
**Adapted from James Agate**

**Enthusiasm:** *n.* naive keenness curable by small doses of experience.
**Leonard Rossiter**

**Entrepreneur:** *n.* one who satisfies his own material cravings by catering to those of the public.
**Rick Bayan**

**Equity:** *n.* a term liberally applied in office politics to enforce policies that disadvantage you when you are out of favour. When you are in favour those same policies are circumvented using incantations such as 'performance bonus', 'salary loading', and 'recognition according to merit'.
**Derek Abbott**

**Erratic:** *n.* consistently inconsistent.
**Contributed specially for *The Wickedictionary* by Mills Egan**

**Epic:** *n.* (*literary term*) too long.
**Book of Lies**

**Etc:** *abbr.* an abbreviation inserted into a written text to make others believe that you know more than you actually do.
**Unknown**

**Ethics:** *n.* 1. an unspoken code of decency that once governed most business and professional transactions, at least theoretically.
**Unknown**

**Ethics:** *n.* 2. a fluctuating commodity that declines in direct proportion to the amount of money at stake.
**Rick Bayan**

**Ethics:** *n.* 3. the best reasons in the world why people should think like you do.
**Contributed specially for *The Wickedictionary* by Lloyd Irving**

**Etiquette:** *n.* a social code devised and memorized by members of the upper classes for the purpose of screening out raffish pretenders to their ranks.
**Rick Bayan**

**Erogenous zone:** *n.* by current reckoning, any region of the human topography with the possible exception of the elbows.
**Rick Bayan**

**Estimate:** *n.* an amount approximately equal to half the eventual cost.
**Unknown**

**Euphemism:** *n.* a figure of speech in which the speaker or writer makes his expression a good deal softer than the facts would warrant him in doing.
**Ambrose Bierce**

**Euthanasia:** *n.* the art of persuading elderly loaded relatives to bring their wills into effect.
**Unknown**

**Exaggeration:** *n.* 1. truth that has lost its temper.
**Khalil Gibran**

**Exaggeration:** *n.* 2. a legitimate literary device to draw attention to the truth.
**Derek Abbott**

**Excuse:** *n.* is a perfectly good reason that has been rejected by those in authority.
**Derek Abbott**

**Experience:** *n.* 1. the name everyone gives to their mistakes.
**Oscar Wilde**

**Experience:** *n.* 2. the ability to repeat one's mistakes with ever-increasing confidence.
**Patrick Hoyte**

**Experience:** *n.* 3. something you don't get until just after you need it.
**Steven Wright**

**Experiment:** *n.* the fine art of fudging scientific data so that they mesh with one's original hypothesis.
**Rick Bayan**

**Expert:** *n.* 1. a person sufficiently jaded with all the facts that he declares when something cannot be done.
**Derek Abbott**

**Expert:** *n.* 2. a person who avoids the small errors while sweeping on to the grand fallacy.
**Steven Weinberg**

**Expert:** *n.* 3. a person who is more than 50 miles from home, has no responsibility for implementing the advice he gives, and shows slides.
**Edwin Meese**

**Expert:** *n.* 4. a person who knows more and more about less and less until he knows absolutely everything about nothing.
**Unknown**

**Expert:** *n.* 5. the last audible voice saying it can't be done, if the world were to blow itself up.
**Peter Ustinov**

**Explanation:** *n.* 1. (*scientific term*) condensed descriptions.
**Attributed to Ernst Mach**

**Explanation:** *n.* 2. (*scientific term*) merely something that provides a logical link between something surprising and something so commonplace that you have not previously thought about it.

**Robert Eugene Bogner**

**Explanation:** *n.* 3. (*scientific term*) something that merely appeases your curiosity, but is really no explanation at all.

**Derek Abbott**

**Explanation:** *n.* 4. (*scientific term*) a scientific explanation is just a form of accountant's balance sheet. It clearly shows how everything adds up to the final number, but it never really tells you why the universe got you into such bad debt in the first place.

**Derek Abbott**

**Explanation:** *n.* 5. (*scientific term*) that which merely leads to more questions like a never ending sequence of Russian dolls.

**Derek Abbott**

**Extremist:** *n.* a conservative of a different ideology to yours.

**Derek Abbott**

# F

**Facebook:** *n.* a social networking website that brings people spread over a large metropolis all the advantages of a close-knit community, including lack of privacy.
**Derek Abbott**

**Fact:** *n.* 1. a folly committed by enough of the right people to confer on it the badge of status.
**Adapted from Rick Bayan**

**Fact:** *n.* 2. information gathered with great accuracy, only to be distorted later.
**Unknown**

**Factionalism:** *n.* the abiding human need to create group conflicts based on religion, politics, race, gender, class or whether toilet paper should be pulled over or under the roll.
**Rick Bayan**

**Fail** *n.* to overachieve at getting low scores.
**Contributed specially for *The Wickedictionary* by Rach Shagwell**

**Faith:** *n.* 1. an illogical belief in the occurrence of the improbable.
**H. L. Mencken**

**Faith:** *n.* 2. an oasis in the heart which will never be reached by the caravan of thinking.
**Khalil Gibran**

**Faith:** *n.* 3. our normal mode of operation, until we punctuate it with odd moments of reason.
**Derek Abbott**

**Faith:** *n.* 4. not wanting to know what is true.
**Friedrich Nietzsche**

**Fascism:** *n.* nationalism with obsessive-compulsive tendencies.
**Rick Bayan**

**Fashion:** *n.* 1. a form of ugliness so intolerable that we have to alter it every six months.
**Oscar Wilde**

**Fashion:** *n.* 2. a means of expressing one's individuality by wearing and doing exactly the same things as others.
**Neil Jones**

**Fashion:** *n.* 3. that which is unwearable until everyone else is wearing it, by which time it is unfashionable.
**Leonard Rossiter**

**Fashion:** *n.* 4. a clothing epidemic.
**Unknown**

**Fatherhood:** *n.* is pretending the present you love most is soap-on-a-rope.
**Bill Cosby**

**Federal budget:** *n.* in the U.S., a miraculous machine that continually cranks out more money than it takes in; unfortunately not yet licensed for use in the home.
**Rick Bayan**

**Felon:** *n.* a person of greater enterprise than discretion, which in embracing an opportunity has formed an unfortunate attachment.
**Ambrose Bierce**

**Female:** *n.* in biology, the thing that is more likely to bite you.
**Adapted from Desmond Morris**

**Feminism:** *n.* 1. is complaining about the male representation of God, whilst overlooking the male representation of the devil. This selectivity extends to altering moot words such as 'chairman' and 'mankind', whilst rather cunningly retaining 'henchman' and 'manslaughter'.
**Derek Abbott**

**Feminism:** *n.* 2. a movement created to allow ugly women access to the mainstream of society.
**Rush Limbaugh**

**Feminism:** *n.* 3. a militant over-reaction to a historically male narrative.
**Contributed specially for *The Wickedictionary* by Karen Rossiter**

**Feminist:** *n.* a woman who intends to fulfil her destiny by aping the worst traits of her oppressors.
**Rick Bayan**

**Fidelity:** *n.* failure to share.
**Derek Abbott**

**Finance:** *n.* the art of passing money from hand to hand until it finally disappears.
**Robert W. Sarnoff**

**Fine:** *n.* a tax for doing wrong as opposed to a tax, which is a fine for doing well.
**Unknown**

**Fishing:** *n.* a venerable contest in which modern man pits his intelligence and technology against the native wit of primitive aquatic vertebrates, and generally finishes second.
**Rick Bayan**

**Flashlight:** *n.* a case for storing dead batteries and light bulbs.
**Unknown**

**Flattery:** *n.* a gift-wrapped insult.
**Unknown**

**Flexibility:** *n.* capacity to contradict your principles.
**Adapted from Jonathan Lynn and Anthony Jay**

**Flying:** *adj.* is learning how to throw yourself at the ground and miss.
**Douglas Adams**

**Focus:** *n.* lack of appreciation of the bigger picture.
**Derek Abbott**

**Food:** *n.* an important part of a balanced diet.
**Fran Lebowitz**

**Food chain:** *n.* the vast hierarchy of predators, with plankton at the bottom and marketing executives at the top.
**Rick Bayan**

**Fool:** *n.* 1. a condition a man may not be aware of, until he is constantly reminded of it after marriage.
**Adapted from H. L. Mencken**

**Fool:** *n.* 2. one who announces loudly that he doesn't suffer others like him gladly.
**Unknown**

**Foolproof:** *n.* an ideal that cannot be attained in the presence of a sufficiently talented fool.
**Unknown**

**Forgiveness:** *n.* that which is inspired by revenge.
**Adapted from Scott Adams**

**Foundation grant:** *n.* a bourgeois beneficence that enables unmarketable artists to continue expressing their contempt for bourgeois values.
**Rick Bayan**

**Franchise:** *n.* a form of business that aims at internationally spawning clones of itself for world domination, providing goods and services that are meticulously consistent in quality. Consistently bad.
**Derek Abbott**

**Freedom:** *n.* 1. in the U.S., the sacred right to speak and act according to one's conscience, except when dealing with sensitive special-interest groups or militant Republican administrations.
**Rick Bayan**

**Freedom:** *n.* 2. a man's natural power of doing what he pleases, so far as he is not prevented by force or law.
**Marcus Tullius Cicero**

**Freedom:** *n.* 3. what the U.S. frequently exports to developing nations, by force if necessary.
**Rick Bayan**

**Freedom:** *n.* 4. the absence of choice.
**Traditional Sufi adage**

**French:** *n.* a race of people who take perverse pleasure in designing car engines completely differently from the British.
**Derek Abbott**

**Friend:** *n.* 1. is one who knows all about you, and still likes you.
**Elbert Hubbard**

**Friend:** *n.* 2. not necessarily one of the people you like best, but merely one of those who got there first.
**Adapted from Peter Ustinov**

**Friendless:** *n.* addicted to utterance of truth and common sense.
**Adapted from Ambrose Bierce**

**Freudian slip:** *n.* when you say one thing and mean your mother.
**Unknown**

**Fun:** *n.* a form of enjoyment that advertising agencies would have you believe everyone, except yourself, is having.
**Tobias Reynolds**

**Fundamentalist:** *n.* 1. a person self-imprisoned on a railway platform, who missed the train of life whilst arguing over really important things such as different interpretations of the station timetable.
**Derek Abbott**

**Fundamentalist:** *n.* 2. in the US, one who is vehemently opposed to the suggestion of any hereditary descendence from an ape and yet behaves like one in matters of foreign policy.
**Derek Abbott**

**Fundamentalist:** *n.* 3. one whose fear of uncertainty extends to his fear of diversity.
**Derek Abbott**

**Fundamentalist:** *n.* 4. in the US, one who accepts a literal interpretation of 100% of the Bible apart from those sections where Jesus behaves like a danged socialist hippy.
**Derek Abbott**

**Fundamentalist:** *n.* 5. one who believes the earth is only 6000 years old and is not amused by that joker who planted all them dinosaur bones.
**Derek Abbott**

**Future generations:** *n. pl.* those to which we will never have to answer and which are now powerless to defend their interests.
**William F. Pickard**

# G

**Gambler:** *n.* one who picks his own pocket.
**Unknown**

**Gambling:** *n.* a tax on the mathematically impaired.
**Jim Auster**

**Geek:** *n.* 1. a person whose experience of lingerie is limited to shop windows and catalogues. Geeks divide their own clothes into two piles—filthy, and filthy but wearable.
**Isham Research**

**Geek:** *n.* 2. a dateless bespectacled engineering student who is constantly spurned by girls, but then later in life has to reluctantly turn down scores of marriage proposals from top fashion models after selling his latest dot-com enterprise for a few billion.
**Derek Abbott**

**Genealogy:** *n.* an account of one's descent from an ancestor who did not particularly care to trace his own.
**Ambrose Bierce**

**Genius:** *n.* one who is clever enough to ensure no one is watching when he luckily stumbles on a good idea.
**Derek Abbott**

**Gentleman:** *n.* 1. formerly the male exemplar of honour, nobility and other behavioural relics from the Age of Chivalry; now dismissed as someone with a testosterone deficiency.
**Unknown**

**Gentleman:** *n.* 2. a gentleman is simply a patient wolf.
**Lana Turner**

**Ghost:** *n.* the outward and visible sign of an inward fear.
**Unknown**

**Gifted children:** *n. pl.* unfortunate tykes who lack the good sense to hide their talents from overly ambitious parents.
**Rick Bayan**

**Gigolo:** *n.* a man whose reputation has been eagerly created by numerous individual women, and yet meets with their collective disapproval.
**Derek Abbott**

**Girlfriend:** *n.* a man's future ex-wife.
**Unknown**

**Global warming:** *n.* a meteorological phenomenon cited to explain the appearance of three consecutive days of fine weather in a British summer.
**Steve Wylie**

**God:** *n.* 1. one who created us in His image, and we have more than reciprocated.
**Adapted from Voltaire**

**God:** *n.* 2. one who answers all prayers, and sometimes with a no.
**Unknown**

**God:** *n.* 3. an omniscient being that even the most hardened atheist gratefully thanks when an unobtainable bombshell of his dreams falls in his lap and professes undying love.
**Derek Abbott**

**Good breeding:** *n.* consists in concealing how much we think of ourselves and how little we think of the other person.
**Mark Twain**

**Good judgment:** *n.* that which comes from experience, and experience comes from bad judgment.
**Rita Mae Brown**

**Gossip:** *n.* a person who will never tell a lie if the truth will do more damage.
**Unknown**

**Government:** *n.* the thing that always gets in no matter who you vote for.
**Unknown**

**Grandparents:** *n.* the people who think your children are wonderful even though they're sure you're not raising them right.
**Unknown**

**Guerrilla:** *n.* what the enemy calls your freedom fighter.
**Derek Abbott**

**Gym:** *n.* a sacred modern temple of self-flagellation that extends one's lifespan for more of the same.
**Derek Abbott**

# H

**Hardware:** *n.* (*computing term*) the equipment used to reveal software faults.
**John Norris**

**Hard work:** *n.* is simply the refuge of people who have nothing whatever to do.
**Oscar Wilde**

**Happiness:** *n.* 1. an agreeable sensation arising from contemplating the misery of another.
**Ambrose Bierce**

**Happiness:** *n.* 2. a form of self-denial about the future, due to an exaggerated sense of satisfaction about the present.
**Derek Abbott**

**Haute cuisine:** *n.* 1. the fine art of serving soup cold on purpose.
**Unknown**

**Haute cuisine:** *n.* 2. a sleight of hand whereby a restaurant charges you more for less.
**Derek Abbott**

**Headache:** *n.* that which is instantly cured by sex and yet prohibits any treatment.
**Derek Abbott**

**Health:** *n.* 1. a delicate equilibrium that may be upset by smoking too many cigarettes or reading too many alarming medical studies.
**Rick Bayan**

**Health:** *n.* 2. is merely the slowest possible rate at which one can die.
**Unknown**

**Health food:** *n.* a family of bland, marginally edible grains, beans, sprouts and other vegetative matter that presumably fortifies the body as effectively as it wilts the spirit.
**Rick Bayan**

**Heaven:** *n.* where the police are British, the lovers are Italian, the mechanics are German, the chefs are French, and it's all organized by the Swiss. As opposed to hell, where the police are German, the chefs are British, the mechanics are French, the lovers are Swiss, and it's all organized by the Italians.
**Unknown**

**Heir:** *n.* the idle offspring of a workaholic.
**Rick Bayan**

**Hell:** *n.* 1. a perpetual holiday.
**George Bernard Shaw**

**Hell:** *n.* 2. Italian punctuality, German humour, and English wine.
**Peter Ustinov**

**Hell:** *n.* 3. eternal torment reserved for the afterlife or available now on an instalment plan, known as marriage.
**Contributed specially for *The Wickedictionary* by L**

**Hermit:** *n.* one with no peer pressure.
**Steve Wright**

**Hero:** *n.* someone who is talented at getting other people killed.
**Joss Wheedon**

**Herpes:** *n.* the affliction of a latter-day leper, rendering the victim untouchable except by fellow sufferers, who must then spend their lives searching for each other like fireflies in the twilight.
**Adapted from Rick Bayan**

**High street:** *n.* a generally imposing thoroughfare running through a district of empty shop fronts.
**Unknown**

**Hip:** *adj.* smartly attuned to the latest cutting-edge clichés.
**Rick Bayan**

**Hipocracy:** *n.* prejudice with a halo.
**Ambrose Bierce**

**Historian:** *n.* 1. an unsuccessful novelist.
**H. L. Mencken**

**Historian:** *n.* 2. one whose future lies in the past.
**Unknown**

**History:** *n.* 1. a fable agreed upon.
**Napoleon**

**History:** *n.* 2. an account of events written down by the winners.
**Adapted from George Orwell**

**History:** *n.* 3. a gallery of pictures in which there are few originals and many copies.
**Alexis de Tocqueville**

**History:** *n.* 4. prophecy backwards.
**Derek Abbott**

**Homophobe:** *n.* someone who projects his own self-hate onto those that are not in self-denial.
**Derek Abbott**

**Hope:** *n.* nature's veil for hiding truth's nakedness.
**Alfred Nobel**

**Horoscope:** *n.* a prediction that is always true due to sufficient generality.
**Derek Abbott**

**Hors d'oeuvres** *n.* a sandwich cut into 20 pieces.
**Unknown**

**Hotel:** *n.* a refuge from home life.
**Adapted from George Bernard Shaw**

**House of Lords:** *n.* in the UK, a body of elderly persons charged with high duties and misdemeanours.
**Leonard Rossiter**

**Human:** *n.* 1. a minor bipedal life form extant on a squalid little planet named Earth, in a backwater little-known galaxy; they are also known as 'Earthlings'. Humans are characterized by an exaggerated sense of self-entitlement, display a collective form of narcissistic personality disorder, and are generally regarded as the rednecks of the universe. Their problems appear to stem from a disingenuous form of business transaction they call 'land ownership.' They are at a primitive stage of development, thankfully can only sense three dimensions, and so are unaware of the rest of us. They are generally thought to be of no threat to the Federation of Planets, as by the time they figure out how to communicate with higher dimensions they will have annihilated themselves anyway. The Federation has blacklisted them as pariahs of the universe and so all funding for academic study of these obnoxious creatures has been suspended for 10 million years or until when their petty factious behaviour ceases, whichever comes soonest.
**Derek Abbott**

**Human:** *n.* 2. one who is almost unique in having the ability to learn from the experience of others, but also remarkable for the apparent disinclination to do so.
**Adapted from Douglas Adams**

**Human:** *n.* 3. one who is smart enough to have ideas but foolish enough to believe them.
**Russ Abbott**

**Human:** *n.* 4. one who does irrational things in the pursuit of phenomenally unlikely payoffs.
**Adapted from Scott Adams**

**Human:** *n.* 5. an ingenious assemblage of portable plumbing.
**Christopher Morley**

**Humans:** *n. pl.* creatures that all look the same and taste like chicken. They even behave like chickens if you put them together in a cage.
**Derek Abbott**

**Human resources:** *n.* corporate nomenclature intended to confer greater dignity on personnel managers while reducing everyone else in the company to the status of bauxite or wood-pulp.
**Rick Bayan**

**Humility:** *n.* a quality that disappears the moment you think you have it.
**Unknown**

**Humor:** *n.* 1. an almost physiological response to fear.
**Kurt Vonnegut**

**Humor:** *n.* 2. a way of holding off how awful life can be.
**Kurt Vonnegut**

**Hunger:** *n.* the best sauce.
**Proverb**

**Hunk:** *n.* a man freely viewed as a sex object by women who refuse to be viewed as such themselves, and generally aren't anyway.
**Rick Bayan**

**Husband:** *n.* a person who empties the waste paper bin and believes that he has cleaned the whole house.
*Chambers Gigglossary*

**Hyperactive children:** *n.* a cheap and relatively clean energy source that might be put to good use after we deplete the planet's supply of fossil fuels.
**Rick Bayan**

**Hypocrisy:** *n.* the vaseline of social intercourse.
**James R. Newman**

**Hypocrite:** *n.* one who nobly disapproves of the despised virtues that he is afflicted with.
**Adapted from Ambrose Bierce**

**Hypochondria:** *n.* the only illness a hypochondriac thinks he doesn't have.

**Unknown**

# I

**Ice age:** *n.* that fateful period which, when approached, causes even the most hardened global warming skeptic to desperately hope that he was wrong.
**Derek Abbott**

**Idea:** *n.* an idea is that which puts the truth in checkmate.
**Adapted from Jose Ortega y Gasset**

**Idealism:** *n.* when men get into trouble by taking their visions and hallucinations too seriously.
**Adapted from H. L. Mencken**

**Ignorance:** *n.* that which is not as vast as our failure to use what we know.
**Adapted from M. King Hubbert**

**Illegal immigrant:** *n.* a hapless foreigner who peacefully enters a country with the noble purpose of propping up its economy, by performing all the jobs that local inhabitants refuse to do, thereby sacrificing himself for the greater good; as opposed to a bloodthirsty foreign warlord who rapes, pillages, and

dominates a country, who with his descendants then gets disingenuously elevated to 'ruling class' status.
**Derek Abbott**

**Imitation:** *n.* the sincerest form of flattery.
**Charles Caleb Colton**

**Immorality:** *n.* the morality of those who are having a better time.
**H. L. Mencken**

**Impossibility:** *n.* that which often has a kind of integrity to it, which the merely improbable lacks.
**Adapted from Douglas Adams**

**Income tax:** *n.* is the hardest thing in the world to understand.
**Albert Einstein**

**Incredulity:** *n.* the difficulty in accepting that a man is telling the truth, when you know that you would lie if you were in his place.
**Adapted from H. L. Mencken**

**Inflation:** *n.* cutting money in half without damaging the paper.
**Unknown**

**Information:** *n.* a somewhat random sequence of symbols that has value to its beholder.
**Derek Abbott**

**Innovation:** *n.* the rediscovery of a forgotten old trick, within a modern context.
**Derek Abbott**

**Insanity:** *n.* 1. doing the same thing, over and over again, but expecting different results.
**Rita Mae Brown**

**Insanity:** *n.* 2. inflation of the ego to its ultimate.
**Phillip K. Dick**

**Insanity:** *n.* 3. the only thing that keeps you sane in a crazy world.
**Adapted from Leo Buscaglia**

**Insurance:** *n.* a form of gambling in which we bet against our chance of escaping disaster, and win only when we lose.
**Rick Bayan**

**Intellect:** *n.* nature's attempt at self-criticism.
**Sir Muhammad Iqbal**

**Intelligence:** *n.* the thing that enables a man to get along without education. Education is the thing that enables a man to get along without the use of his intelligence.
**A. E. Wiggan**

**International relations:** *n.* a questionable view held by a sovereign state that they relate to another sovereign state in a sophisticated and meaningful manner.
**Contributed specially for *The Wickedictionary* by K**

**Internet:** *n.* the most sophisticated technological network ever created, able to link the sum of the world's knowledge and used to share funny pictures of cats.
**Contributed specially for *The Wickedictionary* by Julian O'Shea**

**Intuition:** *n.* a suspension of logic due to impatience.
**Rita Mae Brown**

**IQ:** *n.* the number that predicts the extent to which one will perform successfully on subsequent IQ tests.
**Rick Bayan**

# J

**Jazz:** *n.* 1. music that goes nowhere and finds no resolution—remove any 10-minute sequence and no one will notice the difference.
**Contributed specially for *The Wickedictionary* by Rach Shagwell**

**Jazz:** *n.* 2. music whose notes know no rest, an inflexible order gives birth to them then destroys them, without ever leaving them the chance to recuperate and exist for themselves.
**Jean-Paul Sartre**

**Jet set:** *n.* gypsies with money.
**Rick Bayan**

**Job:** *n.* the ideal gift for a high school or college graduate.
**Evan Esar**

**Joke:** *n.* a form of short story where all the information comes at the end.
**Derek Abbott**

**Judge:** *n.* a law student who marks his own examination papers.
**H. L. Mencken**

**Junk food:** *n.* cheap, satisfying, flavoursome victuals used as a substitute for real food and consisting mainly of salt, fat and sugar, deep-fried to bring out their full atherosclerotic potential.
**Rick Bayan**

**Jury:** *n.* 1. a group of twelve men who, having lied to the judge about their hearing, health and business engagements, have failed to fool him.
**H. L. Mencken**

**Jury:** *n.* 2. a panel of amateurs called upon to decide life-or-death matters in court.
**Rick Bayan**

**Justice:** *n.* a decision in your favour.
**Unknown**

**Just war:** *n.* the theory that nine of the Ten Commandments are inviolate, but that one can be selective when it comes to killing. Under this theory, beliefs in 'just theft' or 'just adultery,' for example, are punishable by hanging or lethal injection.
**Derek Abbott**

# K

**Kill:** *v.t.* to create a vacancy without nominating a successor.
**Ambrose Bierce**

**Killer:** *n.* one who generously risks his life to put the pain of others to an end.
**Unknown**

**Kinetic energy:** *n.* (*scientific term*) that which transfers between colliding objects rather like a ghostly spirit.
**Derek Abbott**

**Kiss:** *v.* to get two people so close together that they can't see anything wrong with each other.
**Unknown**

**Kleptomaniac:** *n.* one who steals for pleasure rather than material gain; a thief with breeding.
**Rick Bayan**

**Knowledge:** *n.* 1. is to know the extent of one's ignorance.
**Confucius**

**Knowledge:** *n.* 2. a slightly better grade of ignorance.
**Derek Abbott**

# L

**Language:** *n.* 1. a tool for concealing the truth.
**Adapted from Charles-Maurice Talleyrand by George Carlin**

**Language:** *n.* 2. that which man invented to satisfy his deep need to complain.
**Lily Tomlin**

**Language:** *n.* 3. a virus from outer space.
**William S. Burroughs**

**Laptop computer:** *n.* a device invented to force businessmen to work at home, on vacation, and on business trips.
**Unknown**

**Last orders:** *n.* a daily 15-minute period generally used as a rehearsal for the end of the world.
**Unknown**

**Late:** *adj.* arriving after the proper time, thereby selflessly giving a sense of purpose and superiority to those who are inconsiderately punctual.
**Derek Abbott**

**Law:** *n.* that which, in its majestic equality, forbids the rich as well as the poor to sleep under bridges, to beg in the streets, and to steal bread.
**Anatole France**

**Lawyer:** *n.* 1. one who protects us against robbers by taking away the temptation.
**H. L. Mencken**

**Lawyer:** *n.* 2. a personal advocate hired to bend the law on behalf of a paying client; for this reason considered the most suitable background for entry into politics.
**Rick Bayan**

**Lawyer:** *n.* 3. one skilled in circumvention of the law.
**Ambrose Bierce**

**Lawyer:** *n.* 4. an advocate of the highest bidder, in contradistinction to an advocate of ethics.
**Derek Abbott**

**Lawyer:** *n.* 5. a learned gentleman who rescues your estate from your enemies and keeps it himself.
**Henry Brougham**

**Lecher:** *n.* a stud with liver spots.
**Rick Bayan**

**Leftist:** *n.* a liberal who bites.
**Rick Bayan**

**Legal:** *adj.* 1. is what formerly meant lawful; now it means loophole.
**Adapted from Leo Kessler**

**Legal:** *adj.* 2. any action is legal, provided no one is watching.
**Unknown**

**Legend:** *n.* a lie that has attained the dignity of age.
**H. L. Mencken**

**Lesbian:** *n.* a quaint euphemism for a woman who resists the intrusion of a man into her private affairs but concurs with his taste in sex partners.
**Rick Bayan**

**Lesbianism:** *n.* a double jeopardy relationship where both parties argue under the influence of PMS.
**Derek Abbott**

**Liar:** *n.* a lawyer on a high commission.
**Adapted from Ambrose Bierce**

**Liberal:** *n.* 1. one who tolerates all beliefs and opinions except those with which he disagrees.
**Rick Bayan**

**Liberal:** *n.* 2. in the US, one who believes in the redistribution of wealth, so long as it's not their wealth that's being distributed.
**Contributed specially for *The Wickedictionary* by Sam Appleton**

**Liberty:** *n.* the right to tell people what they do not want to hear.
**George Orwell**

**Lie:** *n.* 1. an epistemological problem.
**Jonathan Lynn and Anthony Jay**

**Lie:** *n.* 2. economy of truth.
**Unknown**

**Life:** *n.* 1. a sexually transmitted disease and invariably fatal.
**Adapted from Neil Gaiman**

**Life:** *n.* 2. is what kills you in the end.
**Adapted from Katharine Hepburn**

**Life:** *n.* 3. is the art of drawing without an eraser.
**John W. Gardner**

**Life:** *n.* 4. a sequence of events one is not prepared for.
**Unknown**

**Life:** *n.* 5. a series of collisions with the future.
**Jose Ortega y Gasset**

**Life:** *n.* 6. a constant oscillation between the sharp horns of dilemmas.
**H. L. Mencken**

**Life:** *n*. 7. the interval between birth and death.
**Unknown**

**Life:** *n*. 8. one long postponement.
**Henry Miller**

**Life:** *n*. 9. a funny thing that occurred on the way to the grave.
**Quentin Crisp**

**Life insurance:** *n*. a contract that keeps you poor all your life so that you can die rich.
**Unknown**

**Literature:** *n*. an insider's newsletter about affairs relating to molecules, of no importance to anything in the Universe but a few molecules who have the disease called 'thought'.
**Kurt Vonnegut**

**Litigation:** *n*. 1. a machine which you go into as a pig and come out of as a sausage.
**Ambrose Bierce**

**Litigation:** *n*. 2. that which filters out bad management, just like evolution filters out bad genes.
**Chelsea Liu**

**Logic:** *n*. 1. the art of thinking and reasoning in strict accordance with the limitations and incapacities of the human misunderstanding.
**Ambrose Bierce**

**Logic:** *n.* 2. the art of going wrong with confidence.
**Joseph Wood Krutch**

**Loser:** *n.* 1. a highly successfully person who impeccably lives up to measures not sanctioned by the majority.
**Derek Abbott**

**Loser:** *n.* 2. anyone too incompetent to master the ways of the world, or too proud.
**Rick Bayan**

**Lost:** *n.* in the US, an interminable TV series proving an exception to the rule that one should never read a spoiler.
**Derek Abbott**

**Love:** 1. *n.* the delusion that one woman differs from another.
**Attributed to H. L. Mencken**

**Love:** 2. *n.* the triumph of imagination over intelligence.
**Attributed to H. L. Mencken**

**Love:** 3. *n.* a temporary insanity curable by marriage.
**Ambrose Bierce**

**Love:** 4. *n.* staying up all night with a sick child, or a healthy adult.
**Unknown**

**Love:** 5. *n.* an endorphin-induced hallucinatory state designed by Mother Nature to trick us into procreation.
**Derek Abbott**

**Love:** 6. *n.* that which conquers all things except poverty and toothache.
**Adapted from Mae West**

**Love:** 7. *n.* a state of perceptual anesthesia—to mistake an ordinary young woman for a goddess.
**H. L. Mencken**

**Love:** 8. *n.* the delightful interval between meeting a beautiful girl and discovering that she looks like a haddock.
**John Barrymore**

**Love:** 9. *n.* is only the dirty trick played on us to achieve continuation of the species.
**W. Somerset Maugham**

**Loyalty scheme:** *n.* a corporate device for limiting customer choice.
**Derek Abbott**

**Luck:** *n.* the explanation for success of those we don't like.
**Adapted from Jean Cocteau**

**Luxury:** *n.* tomorrow's necessity.
**Derek Abbott**

# M

**Machines:** *n. pl.* labour saving devices efficient enough to put humans out of employment, but with the ingenious advantage that they create a sufficient number of problems to employ twice as many to solve them.
**Derek Abbott**

**Mad:** *adj.* affected with a high degree of intellectual independence.
**Ambrose Bierce**

**Maintenance-free:** *adj.* irreparable.
**Isham Research**

**Magic:** *n.* any technology sufficiently advanced that it exceeds your ability to understand how it works.
**Adapted from Arthur C. Clarke and Jony Ive**

**Majority:** *n.* a large group of people who have gotten tired of thinking and have decided to accept somebody else's opinion.
**Unknown**

**Management:** *n.* 1. a class of semi-skilled corporate hirelings whose rise within the organization correlates directly with the amount of work they delegate to their more talented underlings.
**Rick Bayan**

**Management:** *n.* 2. administration.
**Isham Research**

**Management consultancy:** *n.* a highly effective and legally permissible confidence trick.
**Contributed specially for** *The Wickedictionary* **by Joshua Arnold-Foster**

**Manifesto:** *n.* 1. a statement of what you would get up to if you had talent, honour, and principles.
**Unknown**

**Manifesto:** *n.* 2. organized gibberish masquerading as a panacea for all society's ills.
**Leonard Rossiter**

**Marriage:** *n.* 1. the only war in which you sleep with the enemy.
**Francois de La Rochefoucauld**

**Marriage:** *n.* 2. an alliance entered into by a man who can't sleep with the window shut, and a woman who can't sleep with the window open.
**George Bernard Shaw**

**Marriage:** *n.* 3. nature's way of keeping us from fighting with strangers.
**Alan King**

**Marriage:** *n.* 4. is when a woman exchanges the attentions of many men for the inattention of one.
**Adapted from Helen Rowland**

**Marriage:** *n.* 5. the chief cause of divorce.
**Groucho Marx**

**Marriage:** *n.* 6. a situation where a man loses his bachelor's degree and a woman gains her masters.
**Unknown**

**Marriage:** *n.* 7. the demonstration that warfare between the sexes does not work, thus serving as a salient reminder that warfare between the races is equally doomed.
**Derek Abbott**

**Marriage:** *n.* 8. a bond formed by mutual lack of common sense.
**Unknown**

**Marriage:** *n.* 9. that which takes the vastness of all the possibilities lying on the horizon of life, swiftly slaughtering them all to leave just one.
**Derek Abbott**

**Marriage:** *n.* 10. the state or condition of a community consisting of a master, a mistress and two slaves, making in all, two.
**Ambrose Bierce**

**Marriage:** *n.* 11. is where the chain of wedlock is so heavy that it needs two to carry it, and sometimes three.
**Alexandre Dumas**

**Marriage:** *n.* 12. a condition where it is impossible to be a fool and not know it.
**Adapted from H. L. Mencken**

**Marriage:** *n.* 13. a lottery in which men stake their liberty and women their happiness.
**Unknown**

**Marriage:** *n.* 14. game over.
**Unknown**

**Marriage:** *n.* 15. the prerequisite for divorce.
**Derek Abbott**

**Marriage:** *n.* 16. socialism among two people.
**Barbara Ehrenreich**

**Martial arts:** *n.* a family of Asiatic self-defense disciplines consisting largely of sweeping ornamental gestures of the arms and legs; amusing to look at but disappointingly ineffective when one's opponent is armed with a semi-automatic.

**Rick Bayan**

**Martyrdom:** *n.* the only way a man can become famous without ability.

**George Bernard Shaw**

**Mastication:** *n.* gastronomic music performed on the xylophone of the mandibles.

**Contributed specially for *The Wickedictionary* by Lloyd Irving**

**Mathematical proof:** *n.* the demonstration that a proposition is correct with a level of certainty that at least two mathematicians somewhere in the world understand it.

**Derek Abbott**

**Mathematician:** *n.* 1. a device for turning coffee into theorems.

**Paul Erdös**

**Mathematician:** *n.* 2. one well-versed in calculus of the variations, Riemann manifolds, and higher algebras, but who cannot count, do simple arithmetic or balance his accounts.

**Derek Abbott**

**Mathematics:** *n.* 1. a product of the human imagination that sometimes works on simplified models of reality.

**Derek Abbott**

**Mathematics:** *n.* 2. a divine madness of the human spirit, a refuge from the goading urgency of contingent happenings.
**Alfred North Whitehead**

**Mathematics:** *n.* 3. a game played according to certain simple rules with meaningless marks on paper.
**David Hilbert**

**Mathematics**: *n.* 4. the Darwinian struggle for life of ideas that leads to the survival of the concepts which we actually use, often believed to have come to us fully armed with goodness from some mysterious Platonic repository of truths.
**Simon Altmann**

**Maturity:** *n.* 1. the status obtained after a sufficient number of years of immaturity have elapsed.
**Derek Abbott**

**Maturity:** *n.* 2. a state we reach the day we don't need to be lied to about anything.
**Adapted from Frank Yerby**

**Medicine:** *n.* consists in amusing the patient while nature cures the disease.
**Voltaire**

**Memory:** *n.* the thing you forget with.
**Alexander Chase**

**Metaphysics:** *n.* the finding of bad reasons for what we believe upon instinct; but to find these reasons is no less an instinct.
**F. H. Bradley**

**Method actor:** *n.* one who can't act, so instead becomes the character.
**Derek Abbott**

**Milkman:** *n.* the neighbourhood sperm donor.
**Contributed specially for *The Wickedictionary* by Shahnaz S. Khan**

**Military action:** *n.* an ultimate gift to a regime that gives what its hardliners were actively seeking to provoke, in order to unify their own internal divisions.
**Derek Abbott**

**Military intelligence:** *n.* a contradiction in terms.
**Groucho Marx**

**Military justice:** *n.* is to justice what military music is to music.
**Groucho Marx**

**Mime:** *n.* a dramatic device that does little violence to the language.
**Leonard Rossiter**

**Minimalism:** *n.* a rather long word for describing the opposite.
**Derek Abbott**

**Mining:** *n.* the rape of virgin soil, to avoid the monotony of recycling.
**Derek Abbott**

**Miracle:** *n.* 1. a natural law that happens once.
**Unknown**

**Miracle:** *n.* 2. (*scientific term*) when plotting experimental data on a graph, any inexplicable point that is more than a standard deviation from the best fit curve, which cannot be repeated no matter how hard you try, must be a miracle.
**Derek Abbott**

**Misdemeanor:** *n.* an infraction of the law having less dignity than a felony and constituting no claim to admittance into the best criminal society.
**Ambrose Bierce**

**Miser:** *n.* a person who lives poor so that he can die rich.
**Unknown**

**Misogynist:** *n.* a man who hates women as much as women hate one another.
**H. L. Mencken**

**Mission statement:** *n.* a corporate creed passed on to employees so they can remember why they're skipping lunch.
**Rick Bayan**

**Mistake:** *n.* making a mistake is an excellent means for getting everyone's undivided attention.
**Unknown**

**Moderate:** *n.* (*political term*) one who cannot find equilibrium at either end of the political spectrum.
**Derek Abbott**

**Moderation:** *n.* a form of extremism that places a tight grip upon the human impulse.
**Derek Abbott**

**Money:** *n.* a medium of exchange whose chief value lies in the fact that one lives in a world in which it is overestimated.
**Adapted from H. L. Mencken**

**Monogamy:** *n.* bigamy is having a wife too many, monogamy is the same.
**Oscar Wilde**

**Moral indignation:** *n.* jealousy with a halo.
**H. G. Wells**

**Morality:** *n.* the theory that every human act must be either right or wrong, and that 99% of them are wrong.
**H. L. Mencken**

**Morals:** *n.* excuses for not behaving badly.
**Contributed specially for *The Wickedictionary* by Lloyd Irving**

**Mother:** *n.* someone who thinks that the girls who go after her son are brazen and the ones who don't are stupid.
**Unknown**

**Motivation:** *n.* the point reached by individuals when they have put off everything else, including procrastination.
**Contributed specially for *The Wickedictionary* by Julian O'Shea**

**Mugging:** *n.* begging by force.
**Geoff Dyer**

**Multilateralism:** *n.* 1. an attempt to create polite mob rule.
**Contributed specially for *The Wickedictionary* by K**

**Multilateralism:** *n.* 2. a useful form of employment for surplus public servants who wish to live in Paris.
**Contributed specially for *The Wickedictionary* by K**

**Murder:** *v.* the act of killing, unless it is done in large numbers and to the sound of trumpets.
**Adapted from Voltaire**

**Musicologist:** *n.* a man who can read music but can't hear it.
**Sir Thomas Beecham**

**Music video:** *n.* how film-school cinematographers and posturing post-pubescent stars collaborated to keep rock music on artificial life support long after it should have died naturally.
**Rick Bayan**

**Mythology:** *n.* the early primitive beliefs of a society, as opposed to the real account that it invents later.
**Adapted from Ambrose Bierce**

# N

**Nail polish:** *n.* part of an assortment of make-up items such as lipstick, eyeliner, blush, etc. which ironically makes a woman look better whilst making her young daughter look like a 'tramp'.
**Unknown**

**Narcissist:** *n.* one with inflated self-love, having the big advantage that he won't encounter many rivals for his love.
**Unknown**

**Nation:** *n.* 1. a society united by delusions about its ancestry and by common hatred of its neighbors.
**William Ralph Inge**

**Nation:** *n.* 2. that which is born in the hearts of poets, and that which dies in the hands of politicians.
**Adapted from Sir Muhammed Iqbal**

**Nationalism:** *n.* the habit of assuming that human beings can be classified like insects and that whole blocks of millions or tens of millions of people can be confidently labelled "good" or "bad."
**George Orwell**

**Natural disaster:** *n.* like wars and other national emergencies, natural disasters are a Godsend to any government for diverting attention from its failed domestic policies. Also an opportunistic device for implementing new policies that would otherwise never see the light of day.
**Derek Abbott**

**Necessity:** *n.* almost any luxury you see in the house of a neighbour.
**Unknown**

**Neighbour:** *n.* one whom we are commanded to love as ourselves, and who does all he knows how to make us disobedient.
**Ambrose Bierce**

**Nepotism:** *n.* a sincere belief that charity begins at home.
**Derek Abbott**

**Nerd:** *n.* a person who uses the telephone to talk to other people about telephones.
**Douglas Adams**

**Nerds:** *n. pl.* a race of socially inept, fashion-challenged technophiles that are venerated as it is they that inheriteth the Earth.
**Derek Abbott**

**Neurotic:** *n.* someone who worries about things that didn't happen in the past instead of worrying about something that won't happen in the future, like normal people.
**Unknown**

**Neurotics:** *n. pl.* neurotics are a rabble, good only to support us financially and to allow us to learn from their cases.
**Sigmund Freud**

**Newspaper:** *n.* a device for making the ignorant more ignorant and the crazy crazier.
**H. L. Mencken**

**No:** *n.* it is recommended that we set up an interdepartmental committee with fairly broad terms of reference so that at the end of the day we would be in a position to think through all the implications and take a decision based on long-term considerations rather than rush prematurely into precipitate and possibly ill-conceived action that might well have unforeseen circumstances.
**Jonathan Lynn and Anthony Jay**

**Nominee:** *n.* a modest person shrinking from the distinction of private life and diligently seeking the dishonorable obscurity of public office.
**Ambrose Bierce**

**Normal:** *n.* the average of deviance.
**Rita Mae Brown**

**Nostalgia:** *n.* fond thoughts of imaginary times gone past.
**Leonard Rossiter**

**Notoriety:** *n.* the fame of one's competitor.
**Ambrose Bierce**

**Novel:** *n.* a well-padded short story.
**Ambrose Bierce**

**Nuclear power station:** *n.* an economical way of creating a nuclear weapons infrastructure, at the expense of uneconomical electricity for the masses.
**Derek Abbott**

**Nuclear war:** *n.* that in which all men are cremated equal.
**Dexter Gordon**

**Nuclear weapon:** *n.* 1. a means of bringing about ultimate peace—the cherished peace of silence that total annihilation thankfully brings.
**Derek Abbott**

**Nuclear weapon:** *n.* 2. an agency reserved for use by the most civilized nations for the settlement of disputes that might become troublesome if left unadjusted. Unfortunately, too many formerly uncivilized nations are becoming civilized.

**Leonard Rossiter**

**Nymphomaniac:** *n.* 1. a woman as obsessed with sex as an average man.

**Mignon McLaughlin**

**Nymphomaniac:** *n.* 2. the focus of every man's earnest daily prayer request, which when granted changes the prayer to a good night's sleep.

**Derek Abbott**

**Oats:** *n.* a grain which in England is generally given to horses, but in Scotland supports the people.
**Samuel Johnson**

**Observatory:** *n.* a place where astronomers conjecture away the guesses of their predecessors.
**Ambrose Bierce**

**Obsession:** *n.* commitment with fervour.
**Derek Abbott**

**Obsessive compulsive:** *adj.* highly focussed.
**Derek Abbott**

**Obvious:** *n.* that which is never seen until someone expresses it simply.
**Khalil Gibran**

**Office:** *n.* 1. a place where you relax after your strenuous home life.
**Unknown**

**Office:** *n.* 2. a clean, functional, brightly lit cell inhabited five days a week by diligent souls who forfeit their lives to make a living.
**Rick Bayan**

**Office politics:** *n.* a system of secret alliances, treacherous intrigues, backstabbings, and petty rivalries designed to relieve the tedium of corporate life. The chief legacy of Byzantine civilization in the Western world, appropriately modified for our times; instead of blinding or maiming one's rivals, one simply mutilates their egos.
**Rick Bayan**

**Oil:** *n.* 1. the flammable liquid residue of fossilized prehistoric plants and beasts, found to be suitable for fueling engines and Middle East conflicts.
**Rick Bayan**

**Oil:** *n.* 2. The excrement of the Devil.
**Unknown**

**Old age:** *n.* 1. when regrets take the place of dreams.
**Adapted from John Barrymore**

**Old age:** *n.* 2. is fifteen years older than I am.
**Oliver Wendell Holmes**

**Old age:** *n.* 3. is when competence is a turn on.
**Billy Joel**

**Online:** *n.* (*computing term*) offlife.
**Rick Bayan**

**Opinion:** *n.* what seems to one to be probably true.
*Chamber's Dictionary*, **1952 Edition**

**Ontology:** *n.* the theory that there are multiple universes with only one having the property of existence.
**Unknown**

**Opportunist:** *n.* a person who starts taking a bath if he accidentally falls into a river.
**Unknown**

**Opportunity:** *n.* that which comes brilliantly disguised as an insoluble problem.
**John W. Gardner**

**Opposition:** *n.* in politics, the party that prevents the Government from running amuck by hamstringing it.
**Ambrose Bierce**

**Optimism:** *n.* 1. is inevitably the last hope of the defeated.
**Albert Meltzer**

**Optimism:** *n.* 2. the madness of insisting that all is well when we are miserable.
**Voltaire**

**Optimist:** *n.* 1. one who believes the inevitable will be postponed.
**Adapted from Kin Hubbard**

**Optimist:** *n.* 2. one who has never had much experience.
**Don Marquis**

**Optimist:** *n.* 3. one who doesn't have the patience to worry.
**Derek Abbott**

**Oratory:** *n.* a conspiracy between speech and action to cheat the understanding.
**Ambrose Bierce**

**Orchestra:** *n.* an overgrown chamber ensemble.
**Derek Abbott**

**Order:** *n.* is merely the prevailing form of chaos.
**Kerry Thornley**

**Organ donor:** *n.* someone who looks forward to being outlived by his liver.
**Rick Bayan**

**Originality:** *n.* judicious imitation.
**Voltaire**

**Orthodoxy:** *n.* the ability to say two and two make five when faith requires it.
**George Orwell**

**Ownership:** *n.* the result of a business transaction that gives you the right to hold onto the illusion that a tiny piece of the planet belongs to you.

**Derek Abbott**

# P

**Pacifist:** *n.* one who does not kill his enemies, but reads their obituaries with great pleasure.
**Adapted from Clarence Darrow**

**Pain:** *n.* an uncomfortable frame of mind that may have a physical basis in something that is being done to the body, or may be purely mental, caused by the good fortune of another.
**Ambrose Bierce**

**Panic room:** *n.* a secure room within a building, designed as a refuge from threats such as severe weather, nuclear attack or disgruntled employees.
***Chamber's Dictionary*, 2008 edition**

**Passport:** *n.* a document treacherously inflicted upon a citizen going abroad, exposing him as an alien and pointing him out for special reprobation and outrage.
**Ambrose Bierce**

**Paradox:** *n.* 1. a conflict between reality and your feeling of what reality 'ought to be.'
**Richard Feynman**

**Paradox:** *n.* 2. a paradox is nothing else than grandiose thoughts in embryo.
**Søren Kierkegaard**

**Parallel:** *adj.* (*computing term*) being or pertaining to everything going wrong at once.
**Isham Research**

**Paranoia:** *n.* 1. the pathological belief that one is important enough to be the object of a conspiracy.
**Rick Bayan**

**Paranoia:** *n.* 2. the unreasonable belief that others actually have the time, vast sums of money, and telepathic powers to so perfectly tweak all one's pet annoyances.
**Derek Abbott**

**Paranoid:** *adj.* a paranoid person is one who is open to all the possibilities.
**Contributed specially for *The Wickedictionary* by Mills Egan**

**Patience:** *n.* a minor form of despair, disguised as a virtue.
**Ambrose Bierce**

**Patriot:** *n.* 1. one who gets a parking ticket and rejoices that the system works.
**Unknown**

**Patriot:** *n.* 2. one who is ready to defend his country against his government.
**Edward Abbey**

**Patriot:** *n.* 3. one to whom the interests of a part seem superior to those of the whole. The dupe of statesmen and the tool of conquerors.
**Ambrose Bierce**

**Patriotism:** *n.* 1. the virtue of the vicious.
**Oscar Wilde**

**Patriotism:** *n.* 2. fundamentally, a conviction that a particular country is the best in the world because you were born in it.
**George Bernard Shaw**

**Patriotism:** *n.* 3. the willingness to kill and be killed for trivial reasons.
**Bertrand Russell**

**Patriotism:** *n.* 4. is often an arbitrary veneration of real estate above principles.
**George Jean Nathan**

**Patriotism:** *n.* 5. is supporting your country all the time, and your government when it deserves it.
**Mark Twain**

**Patriotism:** *n.* 6. a dreadful indignity whereby a soul is controlled by geography.
**Adapted from George Santaya**

**Peace:** *n.* 1. in international affairs, a period of cheating between two periods of fighting.
**Ambrose Bierce**

**Peace:** *n.* 2. that which cannot be learned by killing each other's children.
**Adapted from Jimmy Carter**

**Peace treaty:** *n.* that which occurs after many generations of squabbling and fighting; but would only take two minutes to sign if armies, on both sides, gave their weapons to the politicians and told them to slug it out on their own.
**Derek Abbott**

**Perfection:** *n.* that which is achieved, not when there is nothing left to add, but when there is nothing left to take away.
**Antoine de Saint-Exupéry**

**Perfume:** *n.* a pungent liquid manufactured by the megalitre for the female population, serving to reinforce the suspicion that the dividing line between the fragrance of heavenly nectar and lavatory freshener is a narrow one.
**Derek Abbott**

**Perplexity:** *n.* the beginning of knowledge.
**Khalil Gibran**

**Personal floatation device:** *n.* an air filled jacket that saves your life should an aircraft land in water. Demonstrated with great zeal by the crew at the beginning of every flight, even if the flight path is over land only.
**Derek Abbott**

**Personality disorder:** *n.* 1. eccentricity with true commitment.
**Derek Abbott**

**Personality disorder:** *n.* 2. a guarantee against boredom.
**Derek Abbott**

**Pessimist:** *n.* 1. someone who's never happy unless he's miserable.
**Unknown**

**Pessimist:** *n.* 2. someone who wears suspenders as well as a belt.
**Unknown**

**Pessimist:** *n.* 3. one who would complain about the noise if opportunity knocked.
**Unknown**

**Pessimist:** *n.* 4. a man who thinks everybody is as nasty as himself, and hates them for it.
**George Bernard Shaw**

**Pessimist:** *n.* 5. someone who had to live with an optimist.
**Unknown**

**Philanthropist:** *n.* 1. one who selflessly funds vast sums of money to a charitable cause, without drawing attention to himself, but who fails sufficiently to then be recognized as a philanthropist and who then graciously accepts all the tax breaks with absolutely no fanfare at all.
**Derek Abbott**

**Philanthropist:** *n.* 2. one who has trained himself to grin while his conscience is picking his pocket.
**Adapted from Ambrose Bierce**

**Philosopher:** *n.* a fool who torments himself during life, to be spoken of when dead.
**Unknown**

**Philosophy:** *n.* 1. a route of many roads leading from nowhere to nothing.
**Ambrose Bierce**

**Philosophy:** *n.* 2. a game with objectives and no rules. Mathematics is a game with rules and no objectives.
**Unknown**

**Photograph:** *n.* a picture painted by the sun without instruction in art.
**Ambrose Bierce**

**Physicians:** *n. pl.* those that think they do a lot for a patient when they give his disease a name.
**Immanuel Kant**

**Piracy:** *n.* the seaborne plundering of gold, the kidnapping of wenches, or the downloading of movies.
**Contributed specially for** *The Wickedictionary* **by Adam Darius Mistry**

**Plagiarism:** *n.* 1. a literary coincidence where an honorable work is faced with a discreditable priority.
**Adapted from Ambrose Bierce**

**Plagiarism:** *n.* 2. failure to adorn stolen ideas with footnotes, as opposed to scholarship, which repeatedly acknowledges the theft.
**Rick Bayan**

**Plan:** *v.t.* to bother about the best method of accomplishing an accidental result.
**Ambrose Bierce**

**Plastic surgeon:** *n.* a modern high-priest of vanity who offers redemption via a scalpel blade.
**Derek Abbott**

**Platitude:** *n.* an idea (a) that is admitted to be true by everyone, and (b) that is not true.
**H. L. Mencken**

**Platonic love:** *n.* a loaded pistol waiting to go off.
**Unknown**

**Platonism:** *n.* a viral form of philosophical reductionism that breaks apart holistic concepts into imaginary dualisms, thereby generating the insidious inequalities that all mankind's miseries are based upon.
**Derek Abbott**

**Play:** *n.* work that you enjoy doing for nothing.
**Evan Esar**

**Pleasure:** *n.* that which is merely relief.
**Adapted from William S. Burroughs**

**Poetry:** *n.* that which communicates before it is understood.
**Adapted from T. S. Elliot**

**Police arrest***: n.* a rather fortunate situation that generously guarantees lifetime exclusion from jury service.
**Derek Abbott**

**Policy:** *n.* a magic veil that endows corporate bosses and politicians the appearance of acting with consistency, but that can conveniently change its colour like a chameleon when strategic double-talk is required.
**Derek Abbott**

**Politeness:** *n.* the most acceptable hypocrisy.
**Ambrose Bierce**

**Political campaign:** *n.* the best circus ever heard of, with a mass baptism and a couple of hangings thrown in.
**H. L. Mencken**

**Political correctness:** *n.* 1. the ceasing of cognitive abilities relating to rational analysis; often mistaken for religious fundamentalism and/or group think.
**Contributed specially for *The Wickedictionary* by K**

**Political correctness:** *n.* 2. a loss of ability to confront reality in all its diversity. Diversity is instead replaced by an unanimity of meaninglessness.
**Contributed specially for *The Wickedictionary* by K**

**Political correctness:** *n.* 3. the use of inadvertently comical euphemisms mandated by committees of humorless academicians for the purposes of offending no group except believers in free speech.
**Rick Bayan**

**Political speech:** *n.* what you say when you're not saying anything. *See Polite conversation.*
**Contributed specially for *The Wickedictionary* by Lloyd Irving**

**Politician:** *n.* 1. a person with the ability to foretell what is going to happen tomorrow, next week, next month, next year, and has the ability afterward to explain why it didn't happen.
**Winston Churchill**

**Politician:** *n.* 2. one who shakes your hand before elections and your confidence after.
**Unknown**

**Politician:** *n.* 3. a politician is one who thinks of the next election. A statesman, of the next generation.
**Adapted from James Freeman Clarke**

**Politician:** *n.* 4. an ingenious criminal who covers his secret thieving with a pretence of open marauding.
**Adapted from Ambrose Bierce**

**Politician:** *n.* 5. an animal which can sit on a fence and yet keep both ears to the ground.
**H. L. Mencken**

**Politician:** *n.* 6. one who delivers on economy of the truth, rather than truth on the economy.
**Derek Abbott**

**Politician:** *n.* 7. one who is in touch with his inner narcissist.
**Contributed specially for *The Wickedictionary* by Rach Shagwelll**

**Politics:** *n.* 1. a strife of interests masquerading as a contest of principles. The conduct of public affairs for private advantage.
**Ambrose Bierce**

**Politics:** *n.* 2. a pendulum whose swings between anarchy and tyranny are fueled by perpetually rejuvenated illusions.
**Albert Einstein**

**Politics:** *n.* 3. the art of looking for trouble, finding it everywhere, diagnosing it incorrectly and applying the wrong remedies.
**Groucho Marx**

**Politics:** *n.* 4. the entertainment branch of industry.
**Frank Zappa**

**Politics:** *n.* 5. the art of ignoring obvious facts.
**Unknown**

**Pollution:** *n.* the chief product and authenticating sign of civilization.
**Leonard Rossiter**

**Polygamy:** *n.* 1. an act of supreme sacrifice wherein a man risks his life to more than one mother-in-law.
**Derek Abbott**

**Polygamy:** *n.* 2. a house of atonement, or expiatory chapel, fitted with several stools of repentance, as distinguished from monogamy, which has but one.
**Ambrose Bierce**

**Pornography:** *n.* 1. erotica is using a feather, pornography is using the whole chicken.
**Isabel Allende**

**Pornography:** *n.* 2. the truest form of pornography is the depiction of beauty in war.
**Derek Abbott**

**Pornography:** *n.* 3. a satire on human pretensions.
**Angela Carter**

**Pornography:** *n.* 4. a two-dimensional substitute for that which the consumer cannot accomplish in three.
**Rick Bayan**

**Pornography:** *n.* 5. that which excites, whether from approval or disapproval.
**Leonard Rossiter**

**Positive:** *n.* mistaken at the top of one's voice.
**Ambrose Bierce**

**Positive thinking:** *n.* self-improvement through self-deception.
**Rick Bayan**

**Poodle:** *n.* a dog breed often paraded as a living emblem of its owner's wilful lack of taste.
**Unknown**

**Pray:** *v.* to ask that the laws of the universe be annulled on behalf of a single petitioner confessedly unworthy.
**Ambrose Bierce**

**Prejudice:** *n*. 1. a great way of saving time by quickly forming an opinion without bothering to get the facts.
**Unknown**

**Prejudice:** *n*. 2. you are free from prejudice when you hate everyone equally.
**Adapted from W. C. Fields**

**Presidency:** *n*. a cross between a popularity contest and a high school debate, with an encyclopedia of clichés as the first prize.
**Saul Bellow**

**President:** *n*. one who assumes the position of running a country, who if he had any talent at running anything would be earning a lot more running a multinational business empire.
**Derek Abbott**

**Prescription:** *n*. a physician's guess at what will best prolong the situation with least harm to the patient.
**Ambrose Bierce**

**Present:** *n*. 1. an illusory state between immediate past and immediate future.
**Derek Abbott**

**Present:** *n*. 2. that which is pregnant with the future.
**Voltaire**

**Press:** *n.* in the US, a freewheeling clan of news scribes who unofficially elect a president every four years, then conspire to drive him from office.

**Unknown**

**Preventive maintenance:** *n.* a superstitious ritual in which an engineer is allowed to break things and display his inability to fix them in the forlorn hope that this will appease some unknown gods.

**Isham Research**

**Prig:** *n.* a fellow who is always making you a present of his opinions.

**George Eliot**

**Prison:** *n.* a governmental cost-cutting measure, carried out by ostensibly rehabilitating serial killers and petty offenders all under the same roof.

**Derek Abbott**

**Problem:** *n.* that which cannot be solved by the level of thinking that created it.

**Albert Einstein**

**Procrastination:** *n.* 1. the art of keeping up with yesterday.

**George Carlin**

**Procrastination:** *n.* 2. the immediate minimization of excessive hastiness.

**Derek Abbott**

**Procrastination:** *n.* 3. strategic delay.
**Derek Abbott**

**Professional:** *n.* 1. in personal ads, the most desirable sort of potential mate. 2. In the streets, a prostitute. 3. In the business world, see definition #2.
**Rick Bayan**

**Programming:** *n.* (*computing term*) the art of adding bugs to an empty text file.
**Louis Srygley**

**Prohibitionist:** *n.* the sort of man one couldn't care to drink with, even if he drank.
**H. L. Mencken**

**Proof:** *n.* evidence having a shade more plausibility than of unlikelihood. The testimony of two credible witnesses as opposed to that of only one.
**Ambrose Bierce**

**Propaganda:** *n.* 1. patriotism as practiced by our enemies.
**Rick Bayan**

**Propaganda:** *n.* 2. is to a democracy what the bludgeon is to a totalitarian state.
**Noam Chomsky**

**Prophecy:** *n.* the art of selling one's credibility for future delivery.
**Ambrose Bierce**

**Proposal:** *n.* a proposition that lost its nerve.
**Unknown**

**Prostitution:** *n.* 1. a business transaction where one's body is hired out at a much greater price than for what people commonly sell their souls for in a lifetime.
**Derek Abbott**

**Prostitution:** *n.* 2. the only business in the world where the amateurs are better than the professionals.
**Unknown**

**Proverb:** *n.* for a witticism of unknown attribution, the label 'proverb' is what replaces the label 'anon' after a sufficient number of centuries have elapsed.
**Derek Abbott**

**Prude:** *n.* a bawd hiding behind the back of her demeanor.
**Ambrose Bierce**

**Psychiatrist:** *n.* one who asks a lot of expensive questions that your wife asks for nothing.
**Joey Adams**

**Psychologist** *n.* mind stalker.
**Contributed specially for *The Wickedictionary* by Rach Shagwell**

**Pub:** *n.* husband crèche.
**From a sign outside the *King's Head* pub, London, UK**

**Public opinion:** *n.* what people think people think.
**Unknown**

**Public relations:** *n.* propaganda for hire.
**Rick Bayan**

**Punctuality:** *n.* being on time; with the disadvantage that there is nobody there to appreciate it.
**Adapted from Lettice Philpots**

**Puritanism:** *n.* the haunting fear that someone, somewhere, may be happy.
**H. L. Mencken**

# Q

**Quagmire:** *n.* any situation more easily entered into than exited from.
**Adapted from Ambrose Bierce**

**Quantum particles:** *n.* the dreams that stuff is made of.
**Unknown**

**Question:** *n.* a veiled statement that would otherwise be met with ridicule.
**Derek Abbott**

**Quorum:** *n.* a sufficient number of members of a group to have their own way.
**Rick Bayan**

**Quota:** *n.* (*computing term*) the remaining amount of hard disk space your computer thinks it has.
**Derek Abbott**

# R

**Radical:** *n.* a man with both feet planted firmly in the air.
**Franklin Delano Roosevelt**

**Random choice:** *n.* an improvement on management decisions.
**Adapted from Scott Adams**

**Randomness:** *n.* a hidden order, where the key to its decypherment is lost or unknown.
**Derek Abbott**

**Randomness:** *n.* (*mathematical term*) the most ordered way to avoid redundancy.
**Derek Abbott**

**Reality:** *n.* 1. that which, when you stop believing in it, doesn't go away.
**Philip K. Dick**

**Reality:** *n.* 2. an illusion caused by the lack of drugs.
**Unknown**

**Reality:** *n.* 3. that which very few people have the imagination for.
**Adapted from Johann Wolfgang von Goethe**

**Reason:** *n.* pretext.
**Jonathan Lynn and Anthony Jay**

**Reconsider:** *v.* to seek justification for a decision already made.
**Ambrose Bierce**

**Redneck:** *n.* one who's cultural breadth is about as large as his genetic pool.
**Derek Abbott**

**Refuse:** *v.* to refuse awards is another way of accepting them with more noise than is normal.
**Peter Ustinov**

**Relationship:** *n.* that which is easiest with ten thousand people, the hardest is with one.
**Adapted from Joan Baez**

**Relative:** *n.* a grotesque caricature of oneself.
**Adapted from H. L. Mencken**

**Religion:** *n.* 1. the sincere belief that a supreme being has the slightest bit of interest in supremely anthropocentric rituals.
**Contributed specially for *The Wickedictionary* by James Chappell**

**Religion:** *n.* 2. what keeps the poor from murdering the rich
**Napoleon Bonaparte**

**Religion:** *n.* 3. a spiritual straight-jacket.
**Contributed specially for *The Wickedictionary* by L**

**Remarriage:** *n.* the triumph of hope over experience.
**Unknown**

**Remorse:** *n.* regret that one waited so long to do it.
**H. L. Mencken**

**Republican:** *n.* 1. in the US, a creature that remains after all humanity is removed from a politician.
**Contributed specially for *The Wickedictionary* by Ron Berti**

**Republican:** *n.* 2. in the US, the party that says government doesn't work, and then they get elected and prove it.
**P. J. O'Rourke**

**Research:** *n.* if you steal from one author it's plagiarism; if you steal from many it's research.
**Wilson Mizner**

**Resolute:** *adj.* obstinate in an approved manner.
**Adapted from Ambrose Bierce**

**Retainer:** *n.* a bribe below $100,000, as opposed to an 'ex-gratia payment' that is a bribe between $100,000

and $500,000 or an 'advance against profit sharing' that is a bribe over $500,000.
**Adapted from Jonathan Lynn and Anthony Jay**

**Reproduction:** *n.* the division of amoebas, the pollination of plants, the rutting of wildebeest, and the drunken frenzied Friday nights of humans.
**Derek Abbott**

**Revelry:** *n.* the sound of people pretending to have a good time.
**Unknown**

**Revolution:** *n.* that which evaporates and leaves behind the slime of a new bureaucracy.
**Adapted from Franz Kafka**

**Rich:** *n.* becoming rich is the best way to finding missing relatives.
**Unknown**

**Rite:** *n.* a religious or semi-religious ceremony fixed by law, precept or custom, with the essential oil of sincerity carefully squeezed out of it.
**Ambrose Bierce**

**Robber:** *n.* one whose careful planning and execution of a heist is much more demanding and pays much less than dropping his ethical standards by being gainfully employed as a lawyer.
**Derek Abbott**

**Romance:** *n.* that which begins with a prince kissing an angel, and ends with a bald headed man yawning at a fat woman.

**Evan Esar**

# S

**Safety belt:** *n.* 1. a means for denying transplant patients the body parts they so desperately require.
**Derek Abbott**

**Safety belt:** *n.* 2. on an aircraft, a device that extends your life by precisely two extra seconds as you plummet to the ground precariously strapped to an incinerated piece of fuselage.
**Derek Abbott**

**Safety belt:** *n.* 3. on an aircraft, a means for helping the rescue team to identify your body.
**Contributed specially for *The Wickedictionary* by Withawat Withayachumnankul**

**Saint:** *n.* a dead sinner revised and edited.
**Ambrose Bierce**

**Satanist:** *n.* one who defeats himself by displaying all the noble qualities of loyalty, love, truth, and charity towards fellow satanic brothers.
**Derek Abbott**

**Satire:** *n.* an obsolete kind of literary composition in which the vices and follies of the author's enemies were expounded with imperfect tenderness.
**Ambrose Bierce**

**Sausage:** *n.* essentially a repackaging of the most revolting parts of a dead carcass, sold to the masses as a value-added product. A prime example of how capitalism works.
**Derek Abbott**

**Scandal:** *n.* that which ruins an unpopular official and causes a popular one to enjoy an even higher approval rating.
**Rick Bayan**

**Schadenfreude:** *n.* passive revenge.
**Derek Abbott**

**Schizophrenia:** *n.* a healthy response to a sick society.
**Adapted from Krishnamurti**

**Science:** *n.* 1. the belief in the ignorance of experts.
**Richard Feynman**

**Science:** *n.* 2. organized common sense where many a beautiful theory was killed by an ugly fact.
**Thomas Huxley**

**Science:** *n.* 3. is the road to pertinent answers, found by asking impertinent questions.
**Adapted from Jacob Bronowski**

**Science:** *n.* 4. that in which authority of thousands of opinions is not worth as much as one tiny spark of reason in an individual man.
**Galileo Galilei**

**Science:** *n.* 5. that which does not try to explain, hardly even tries to interpret, but mainly makes models.
**Adapted from John von Neumann**

**Science:** *n.* 6. a modern form of alchemy that produces wealth by producing the understanding for enabling valuable products from base ingredients. Science is merely functional alchemy that has had a few incorrect assumptions fixed, but has in its arrogance replaced them with more insidious ones.
**Derek Abbott**

**Science fiction:** *n.* the improbable made possible, as opposed to fantasy that is the impossible made probable.
**Adapted from Rod Serling**

**Secret:** *n.* something you tell to only one person at a time.
**Unknown**

**Seethe:** *v.* to quietly reflect that many are better than you at everything.
**Unknown**

**Self:** *n.* that which is harder to cheat than the rest of the world.
**George Bernard Shaw**

**Self-esteem:** *n.* the dangling carrot that drives the self-help industry.
**Rick Bayan**

**Selfish:** *adj.* 1. devoid of consideration for the selfishness of others.
**Ambrose Bierce**

**Selfish:** *adj.* 2. a selfish person is one so self-absorbed, providing the consolation that he isn't even aware of all the bad press about you. The guarantee of a loyal friendship.
**Derek Abbott**

**Selfishness:** *n.* is not living as one wishes to live, it is asking others to live as one wishes to live.
**Oscar Wilde**

**Self-respect:** *n.* is the secure feeling that no one, as yet, is suspicious.
**H. L. Mencken**

**Semicolon:** *n.* a transvestite hermaphrodite representing absolutely nothing. All it does is show you've been to college.
**Kurt Vonnegut**

**Seriousness:** *n.* the only refuge of the shallow.
**Oscar Wilde**

**Sex:** *n.* 1. one of the most beautiful, natural, wholesome things that money can buy.
**Tom Clancy**

**Sex:** *n.* 2. a form of Russian roulette that can result in producing a saint or a dictator.
**Derek Abbott**

**Sex:** *n.* 3. the thing that takes up the least amount of time and causes the most amount of trouble.
**John Barrymore**

**Sexual equality:** *n.* a noble ideal that cannot be obtained so long as women persist in requiring ten times more luggage capacity than men on international flights, whilst expecting their husbands to carry the burden.
**Derek Abbott**

**Shin:** *n.* a device for finding furniture in the dark.
**Steven Wright**

**Shopping:** *n.* a retail therapy.
**Unknown**

**Show business:** *n.* sincere insincerity.
**Benny Hill**

**Silence:** *n.* 1. the perfect expression of scorn.
**George Bernard Shaw**

**Silence:** *n.* 2. the period before a child is born and after it goes to college.
**Unknown**

**Silence:** *n.* 3. the voice of complicity.
**Unknown**

**Simplicity:** *n.* the ultimate sophistication.
**Leonardo da Vinci**

**Sin:** *n.* self-expression.
**Adapted from Max Stirner**

**Skeleton:** *n.* a bunch of bones with the person scraped off.
**Unknown**

**Skeptic:** *n.* a true believer in another set of beliefs.
**Phillip E. Johnson**

**Slang:** *n.* language that rolls up its sleeves, spits on its hands, and gets down to work.
**Leonard Rossiter**

**Sloth:** *n.* a condition condemned by those without the imagination to create free time.
**Contributed specially for *The Wickedictionary* by Lloyd Irving**

**Socialism:** *n.* a philosophy of failure, the creed of ignorance, and the gospel of envy, its inherent virtue is the equal sharing of misery.
**Winston Churchill**

**Society:** *n.* that which honours its live conformists and its dead troublemakers.
**Mignon McLaughlin**

**Song:** *n.* 1. the licensed medium for bawling in public things too silly or sacred to be uttered in ordinary speech.
**Oliver Herford**

**Song:** *n.* 2. anything that is too stupid to be spoken.
**Voltaire**

**Software bug:** *n.* a random feature embedded in a perfectly good piece of software.
**Unknown**

**Sorcery:** *n.* the ancient prototype and forerunner of political influence. It was, however, deemed less respectable and sometimes was punished by torture and death.
**Unknown**

**Specialist:** *n.* a man who knows more and more about less and less, according to a generalist. As opposed to a generalist who knows less and less about more and more, according to the specialist.
**Adapted from William J. Mayo**

**Speed dating:** *n.* an opportunity to get over all your disappointments in one batch.
**Unknown**

**Sperm:** *n.* a champion swimmer that disappointingly loses all its ability after it turns into a human.
**Derek Abbott**

**Sperm donor:** *n.* an apathetic rapist who nevertheless achieves his goal of gratuitously filling the genetic pool as widely as possible with his genes.
**Derek Abbott**

**Sports car:** *n.* penis prosthetic.
**Derek Abbott**

**Standard:** *adj.* manufactured by the biggest supplier.
**Isham Research**

**Stalker:** *n.* an admirer whose attentions are unwanted.
**Derek Abbott**

**Stalling:** *n.* creative inertia.
**Jonathan Lynn and Anthony Jay**

**Star:** *n.* a performer who makes more than his or her agent.
**Rick Bayan**

**Statesman:** *n.* a politician who has been dead ten or fifteen years.
**Harry S. Truman**

**Statistician:** *n.* 1. a man who believes figures don't lie, but admits that under analysis some of them won't stand up either.
**Evan Esar**

**Statistician:** *n.* 2. someone who is good with numbers, but lacks the personality to be an accountant.
**Unknown**

**Statistics:** *n.* the science of producing unreliable facts from reliable figures.
**Evan Esar**

**Stilettos:** *n.* precarious high heels that make a man-eater appear vulnerable.
**Derek Abbott**

**Stockbroker:** *n.* one who invests your money until it has all gone.
**Woody Allen**

**Straight line:** *n.* 1. (*scientific term*) the shortest distance between two points, for those who are too lazy to search for a space-time wormhole through the universe.
**Derek Abbott**

**Straight line:** *n.* 2. (*scientific term*) that which can be drawn through any set of data points on a log-log plot over a sufficiently small interval.
**Derek Abbott**

**Strategists:** *n.* a group of people who are getting their act together.
**Unknown**

**Strategy:** *n.* tactics is knowing what to do when there is something to do, whereas strategy is knowing what to do when there is nothing to do.
**Savielly Tartakower**

**Strike:** *n.* industrial inaction.
**Unknown**

**Stupidity:** *n.* a higher form of intelligence perfectly designed to avoid responsibility.
**Derek Abbott**

**Subtlety:** *n.* the art of saying what you think and getting out of the way before it is understood.
**Unknown**

**Success:** *n.* 1. the one unpardonable sin against one's fellows.
**Ambrose Bierce**

**Success:** *n.* 2. the ability to go from one failure to another with no loss of enthusiasm.
**Winston Churchill**

**Success:** *n.* 3. is when a man makes more money than his wife can spend.
**Adapted from Lana Turner**

**Success:** *n.* 4. the most effective form of revenge on one's enemies.
**Derek Abbott**

**Successful:** *adj.* a successful person is merely one who has channelled his obsessive compulsive tendencies to something useful.
**Derek Abbott**

**Suicide:** *n.* is the sincerest form of self-criticism.
**Unknown**

**Sun:** *n.* nature's nuclear fusion reactor that is at an arguably safe distance from Earth; it generously affords us 5000 times our current world energy needs and will run reliably over the next billion years with zero downtime.
**Derek Abbott**

**Sunday school:** *n.* a prison in which children do penance for the evil conscience of their parents.
**H. L. Mencken**

**Superego:** *n.* an advanced state of self-hood reached only by car park attendants and doctors' receptionists.
**Unknown**

**Superglue:** *n.* an adhesive of unparalleled strength. Excellent for gluing fingers together and utterly useless for all else.
**Derek Abbott**

**Superstition:** *n.* 1. a premature explanation that overstays its time.
**George Iles**

**Superstition:** *n.* 2. a belief which leaves no place for doubt.
**José Bergamín**

**Sustainable growth:** *n.* a cheeky little oxymoron suggesting the idea of economic growth that is sustainable over vast ecological time scales; where in practice this is often the time period required to just make it through to the next election.
**Derek Abbott**

**Svelte** *n.* tastefully anorexic.
**Derek Abbott**

**Sweater** *n.* a garment worn by a child when its mother feels chilly.
**Unknown**

**Sympathy:** *n.* is what one woman offers another in exchange for the juicy details.
**Unknown**

**System administrator:** *n.* (*computing term*) a person whose job it is to do everything that isn't his job.
**Alan Silverstein**

**System update:** *n.* (*computing term*) a quick method of trashing all of your software.
**Unknown**

# T

**Table manners:** *n.* a gastronomic ritual invented by the English, so that good manners at least compensates the lack of good cuisine.
**Derek Abbott**

**Tabloid:** *n.* a compact journal filled with tall tales of celebrity infidelities, woes, gaffes, feuds and diseases, so as to minimize mass resentment of their undeserved fame and wealth.
**Unknown**

**Tact:** *n.* the ability to describe others as they see themselves.
**Abraham Lincoln**

**Talk show:** *n.* an opportunity for people to confess to millions of viewers what they would be ashamed to admit to their next-door neighbors.
**Rick Bayan**

**Tariff:** *n.* a scale of taxes on imports, designed to protect the domestic produce against the greed of his consumer.
**Ambrose Bierce**

**Taste:** *n.* a quality possessed by persons without originality or moral courage.
**George Bernard Shaw**

**Tax:** *n.* is what costs you hundreds of dollars when there is a tax increase, but you only save about 30 cents when there is a tax cut.
**Unknown**

**Tax break:** *n.* a desperate attempt at buying votes, particularly when announced close to an election.
**Derek Abbott**

**Teacher:** *n.* a person who talks to himself for a living; as opposed to a lunatic, who talks to himself for fun.
**Unknown**

**Team player:** *n.* the type of cooperative, self-effacing employee beloved by corporations that promote egotists to the top positions.
**Rick Bayan**

**Tears:** *n.* the hydraulic force by which masculine will-power is defeated by feminine water power.
**Unknown**

**Technology:** *n.* 1. a way of organizing the universe so that man doesn't have to experience it.
**Max Fritsch**

**Technology:** *n.* 2. the means by which today's forward-looking companies produce tomorrow's obsolete gadgets.
**Rick Bayan**

**Technophilia:** *n.* the father of invention.
**Unknown**

**Teleconference:** *n.* a way of holding an international meeting without having to smell the French.
**Isham Research**

**Telephone plan:** *n.* a form of indentured slavery, where to buy one's freedom from a telephone company comes at a high cost.
**Derek Abbott**

**Television:** *n.* 1. a more socially acceptable synonym of myopovision.
**Contributed specially for *The Wickedictionary* by Eran Binenbaum**

**Television:** *n.* 2. a tiresome advertising portal punctuated with an occasional movie of interest.
**Derek Abbott**

**Television:** *n.* 3. the orphaned step-child of radio.
**Unknown**

**Temptation:** *n.* 1. that which goes away when you yield to it.
**Adapted from Oscar Wilde**

**Temptation:** *n*. 2. a woman's weapon and man's excuse.
**H. L. Mencken**

**Temptation:** *n*. 3. an irresistible force at work on a movable body.
**H. L. Mencken**

**Thief:** *n*. 1. a petty thief is one you hang, but a truly great thief is one you appoint to public office.
**Adapted from Aesop**

**Thief:** *n*. 2. a person with a fine eye for opportunity.
**Unknown**

**Theology:** *n*. 1. searching in a dark cellar at midnight for a black cat that isn't there.
**Robert A. Heinlein**

**Theology:** *n*. 2. the recitation of the incomprehensible by the unspeakable to pick the pockets of the unthinking.
**Robert Anton Wilson**

**Theory:** *n*. (*scientific term*) is the first term in the Taylor series of practice.
**Thomas M. Cover**

**Thermodynamics:** *n*. (*scientific term*) is just number counting.
**Paul C. W. Davies**

**Thinking:** *n.* a rearrangement of one's prejudices.
**Adapted from William James**

**Time:** *n.* 1. what stops everything from happening all at once.
**John Wheeler**

**Time:** *n.* 2. that which wounds all heels.
**Groucho Marx**

**Time capsule:** *n.* a collection of objects gathered to show our descendants how tasteless and dim-witted we were.
**Unknown**

**Timetable:** *n.* a list that sets out all the times when a train will definitely not be departing on any particular day.
**Unknown**

**Today:** *n.* 1. the most obscure part of history.
**Unknown**

**Today:** *n.* 2. is what will be thought of as part of the Dark Ages.
**Unknown**

**Today:** *n.* 3. the tomorrow that you worried about yesterday.
**Unknown**

**Tolerance:** *n.* 1. the virtue of the man without convictions.
**Gilbert Keith Chesterton**

**Tolerance:** *n.* 2. the respect of another fellow's religion, but only in the sense and to the extent that we respect his theory that his wife is beautiful and his children smart.
**Adapted from H. L. Mencken**

**Tomorrow:** *n.* one of the greatest labour saving devices of today.
**Unknown**

**Transparency:** *n.* refers to the open flow of information between management and the workers. Now done with such zeal that the workers have no time to read the resulting barrage of emails.
**Derek Abbott**

**Trial:** *n.* 1. a contest to see who can afford the cleverest lawyer.
**Derek Abbott**

**Trial:** *n.* 2. a formal inquiry designed to prove and put on record the blameless characters of judges, advocates, and jurors.
**Ambrose Bierce**

**Truth:** *n.* 1. that which begins as a blasphemy.
**George Bernard Shaw**

**Truth:** *n.* 2. that which has only to pass through a few persons to become fiction.

**Evan Esar**

**Truth:** *n.* 3. (*political term*) any statement that can't be proved false.

**Jonathan Lynn and Anthony Jay**

**Tyrant:** *n.* a politician who is no longer concealing his ambitions and intentions.

**Unknown**

# U

**UFO:** *n.* a result of the known irrational characteristics of terrestrial intelligence rather than of the unknown rational efforts of extra-terrestrial intelligence.
**Richard Feynman**

**Ugliness:** *n.* 1. a gift of the gods to certain women, entailing virtue without humility.
**Ambrose Bierce**

**Ugliness:** *n.* 2. the guardian of women.
**Traditional Hebrew adage**

**Unauthorized biography** *n.* an unspoken contract between a biographer and a celebrity for increasing both book sales and welcomed infamy.
**Derek Abbott**

**Uncertainty:** *n.* the thing that makes knowledge interesting.
**Derek Abbott**

**Unemployed:** *n.* between jobs.
**Traditional saying**

**Uniqueness:** *n.* a quality that is not unique itself as everyone has it.
**Derek Abbott**

**United States of America:** *n.* 1. a land founded in 1776 on the principles of life, liberty, and the reckless pursuit of happiness at any cost. America is a place where even the poorest immigrant can, through hard work and dedication, achieve the American Dream for his employer. A nation where any determined individual can climb to the top of the corporate ladder and kick it down so that nobody else can. Where a man can go from rags to riches almost overnight, and from riches back to rags in even less time, then write a book about it, option the rights to a TV network or film studio, and blow all that money on drugs.
**Adapted from *The Onion***

**United States of America:** *n.* 2. a country that celebrates its liberty by freeing its citizens from the imposition of a universal health-care system.
**Derek Abbott**

**Universal:** *n.* does not fit anything properly.
**Unknown**

**Universalist:** *n.* one who forgoes the advantage of a Hell for persons of another faith.
**Ambrose Bierce**

**Universe:** *n.* one of God's practical jokes.
**Unknown**

**University:** *n.* what a college becomes when the faculty loses interest in students.
**John Ciardi**

**University management:** *n.* a group of failed academics.
**Derek Abbott**

**Urinal:** *n.* the one place where all men are peers.
**Rick Bayan**

**Use:** *n.* that which everything has; even uselessness itself.
**Unknown**

**User friendly:** *n.* of or pertaining to any feature, device or concept that makes perfect sense to a programmer.
**Unknown**

**Ultimatum:** *n.* in diplomacy, a last demand before resorting to concessions.
**Ambrose Bierce**

# V

**Vacation:** *n.* a perilous journey usually to a far-flung destination, undertaken in a large flying metal tube with wings. Designed to provide respite and refreshment from one's daily toil, but invariably results in jet lag, dysentery, and extra overtime to pay for the said pleasure.
**Derek Abbott**

**Valentine's Day:** *n.* a mass societal ritual where petrified men manufacture tangible manifestations of undying devotion and where the sinister cabal run by Hallmark, Hershey's, and the National Restaurant Association win out.
**Adaptable from Jordan Rane**

**Vegetarian:** *n.* 1. an old tribal word for 'bad hunter.'
**Unknown**

**Vegetarian:** *n.* 2. a herbivorous individual with Buddhist tendencies. One who rejects the ghoulish concept of forking animal remains down the gullet, preferring to dine upon the corpses of plants and their detachable reproductive organs (popularly known as 'fruit').
**Unknown**

**Veneer:** *n.* a thin, finely finished exterior that effectively conceals the underlying substance; e.g., a mortician's smile or the civility that prevails at a Hollywood party.
**Unknown**

**Viagra:** *n.* a tiny blue pill that stiffens one's resolve to fight against junk email.
**Derek Abbott**

**Victim:** *n.* one who colludes with his own downfall.
**Ian McEwin**

**Victory:** *n.* that which goes to the player who makes the next-to-last mistake.
**Savielly Grigorievitch Tartakower**

**Video camera:** *n.* an audiovisual recording device thrust into the hands of the public so that future social historians might develop migraines looking at our school plays, pet tricks, weddings, and christenings.
**Unknown**

**Video game:** *n.* 1. an electronic form of opium, consumed by stony-eyed young addicts either at home or in dark communal dens, where their families occasionally must venture to retrieve them.
**Unknown**

**Video game:** *n.* 2. that which increases a child's imagination if the game involves Italian plumbers knocking out sentient turtles whilst consuming magic

mushrooms and which increases retardation if a child repeatedly accesses WWII simulations.
**Contributed specially for *The Wickedictionary* by Adam Darius Mistry**

**Virginity:** *n.* the only quality in another person that you want to both find and yet destroy all at the same time.
**Derek Abbott**

**Virtue:** *n.* that which is more enjoyable when a man repents his faults rather than avoiding them.
**Unknown**

**Virtues:** *n. pl.* certain abstentions.
**Ambrose Bierce**

**War:** *n.* 1. is where truth is the first casualty.
**Adapted from Aeschylus**

**War:** *n.* 2. young men dying and old men talking.
**From the film** *Troy* **(2004)**

**War:** *n.* 3. an effort to make the laws of God and nature take sides with one party.
**Henry David Thoreau**

**War:** *n.* 4. a massacre of people who don't know each other for the profit of people who know each other but don't massacre each other.
**Paul Valery**

**War:** *n.* 5. a cowardly escape from the problems of peace.
**Thomas Mann**

**War:** *n.* 6. a device for maintaining peace between nations, which is at least as sustainable as beating one's wife into maintaining a cordial bedroom relationship.
**Derek Abbott**

**War:** *n.* 7. the forced acquisition of what one wants from what another has. *See rape.*
**Contributed specially for *The Wickedictionary* by Adam Darius Mistry**

**War:** *n.* 8. is where the object is not to die for your country, but to make the other bastard die for his.
**George Patton**

**War:** *n.* 9. that which brings peace, but only to its victims.
**Adapted from Leonid S. Sukhorukov**

**War:** *n.* 10. is where fathers bury their sons; as opposed to peace, where sons bury their fathers.
**Adapted from Heroditus**

**War:** *n.* 11. is waged by the rich and it is the poor who die.
**Adapted from Jean-Paul Sartre**

**War:** *n.* 12. a device whereby chaos amplifies religious and ideological differences, numbing the senses, thereby allowing corporate greed to painlessly thrust through the back door and even seem like pleasure.
**Derek Abbott**

**War:** *n.* 13. a form of slave labour, where men work themselves to death for the lords of the military-industrial complex in the faint hope they may someday buy their freedom.
**Derek Abbott**

**War:** *n.* 14. menstruation envy.
**Unknown**

**War:** *n.* 15. an opportunity for governments to use up their weapons arsenal before they become obsolete, so they can justify purchasing the latest upgrades for more of the same.
**Derek Abbott**

**War:** *n.* 16. a brilliant government scheme for addressing declining unemployment figures and avoiding issues of decaying internal infrastructure.
**Derek Abbott**

**War:** *n.* 17. a time-honoured means for an unpopular government to gain public unity through fear by manufacturing a common enemy.
**Derek Abbott**

**War:** *n.* 18. the killing of strangers against whom you feel no personal animosity; strangers whom, in other circumstances, you would help if you found them in trouble, and who would help you if you needed it.
**Mark Twain**

**War hero:** *n.* one who sacrificed his life to failed politicians.
**Derek Abbott**

**Wealth:** *n.* any income that is at least $100 more a year than the income of one's wife's sister's husband.
**H. L. Mencken**

**Weed:** *n.* a spurned plant that is not appreciated for its beauty, nor is bestowed its rightful honour to be eaten.
**Derek Abbott**

**Wedding:** *n.* similar to a funeral except that you get to smell your own flowers.
**Adapted from Grace Hansen**

**Wedding dress:** *n.* a dress coutured with frills and ornamentation sufficient enough to conceal the pregnancy.
**Derek Abbott**

**Wedding ring:** *n.* 1. a subtle signal to single admirers that they should abandon all hope, since the wearer already has.
**Unknown**

**Wedding ring:** *n.* 2. the world's smallest handcuffs.
**Unknown**

**Welfare:** *n.* a public safety net strung up to catch the casualties of the free market system and keep them tangled in the webbing for generations.
**Unknown**

**Welsh:** *n.* a language which, when spoken, sounds like a beautiful song, but when written looks like the alphabet just vomited.
**Adapted from *The Onion***

**Whisky:** *n.* the amber of the gods administered in 700 ml instalments.
**Contributed specially for *The Wickedictionary* by Lloyd Irving**

**Wickedictionary:** *n.* the product of an unholy alliance between Ambrose Bierce and Derek Abbott resulting in an obscene collection of twisted definitions that perversely expose the truth.
**Derek Abbott**

**Wickedness:** *n.* is to create a public scandal, as opposed to sinning in private that is no sin at all.
**Adapted from Molière**

**Wife:** *n.* a woman who has ceased to be your girlfriend and resents anyone attempting to fill the vacancy.
**Dick Chinnery**

**Wikipedia:** *n.* the world's most accurate encyclopedia[citation needed].
**Contributed specially for *The Wickedictionary* by Julian O'Shea**

**Windows 95:** *n.* a 32-bit patch to a 16-bit GUI for an 8-bit operating system written for a 4-bit processor by a 2-bit company that can't stand one bit of competition.
**Isham Research**

**Wine:** *n.* 1. light held together by moisture.
**Galileo Galilei**

**Wine:** *n.* 2. an alcoholic beverage with a rather extreme range in quality. Good wine ruins the pocket; bad wine ruins the stomach. *See Woman.*
**Unknown**

**Wine:** *n.* 3. an overpriced beverage consisting merely of a macerated slurry of pulped grapes, yeast, malic acid, pectinase, sulphur dioxide, and tartaric acid together with the toe jam of a sweaty Frenchman.
**Derek Abbott**

**Winter:** *n.* those long miserable cold days when you begin to wonder who turned off the global warming.
**Derek Abbott**

**Wisdom:** *n.* 1. is the abstract of the past, but beauty is the promise of the future.
**Oliver Wendell Holmes**

**Wisdom:** *n.* 2. the ability to recognize a mistake when you make it again.
**Unknown**

**Wisdom:** *n.* 3. is to know nothing except the fact of one's ignorance.
**Adapted from Socrates**

**Wit:** *n.* educated insolence.
**Aristotle**

**Woman:** *n.* a disease. An ugly woman is a disease of the stomach, a handsome woman a disease of the head.
**Traditional English adage**

**Women:** *n. pl.* 1. those which have hydrofluoric acid bottled up inside.
**Kurt Vonnegut**

**Women:** *n. pl.* 2. those that make highs higher and the lows more frequent.
**Friedrich Nietzsche**

**Women:** *n. pl.* 3. those that don't want to hear what you think. Women want to hear what they think—in a deeper voice.
**Bill Cosby**

**Women:** *n. pl.* 4. those who Nature has given so much power that the law has wisely given them little.
**Samuel Johnson**

**Women:** *n. pl.* 5. the product of two X-chromosomes, as opposed to men who have only one X-chromosome. Thus half of a man is woman and yet this appears insufficient for mutual understanding.
**Derek Abbott**

**Words:** *n. pl.* a device to hide our thoughts.
**Adapted from Voltaire**

**Work:** *n.* the curse of the drinking classes.
**Oscar Wilde**

**World domination:** *n.* the noblest form of megalomania, as it graciously accepts all the problems that come with it.
**Derek Abbott**

**Wrath:** *n.* anger of a superior quality and degree, appropriate to exalted characters and momentous occasions; as, "the Wrath of God,""the day of wrath," etc.
**Ambrose Bierce**

**Wrinkles:** *n.* character lines on other people.
**Unknown**

**Wristwatch:** *n.* a fashion accessory with a clock in the middle, its status value being roughly proportional to the illegibility of the dial.
**Unknown**

# X

**Xenophobia:** *n.* a dislike of those foreign nations that remind us of our own follies.
**Adapted from Socrates.**

**X-ray:** *n.* a diagnostic tool used to detect existing cancerous growths and create new ones for future examinations to reveal.
**Unknown**

# Y

**Yawn:** *n.* an honest opinion openly expressed.
**Unknown**

**Yesterday:** *n.* 1. is but today's memory, and tomorrow is today's dream.
**Khalil Gibran**

**Yesterday:** *n.* 2. what tomorrow will be in two days time.
**Unknown**

**Youth:** *n.* 1. a pristine condition worshiped by menopausal women in sweatsuits and shrinking men with chestnut-brown toupees, while those who actually possess it are frequently too shallow or despondent to appreciate it.
**Rick Bayan**

**Youth:** *n.* 2. an ideal state, if only it came a little later in life.
**Adapted from Herbert Henry Asquit**

# Z

**Zeal:** *n.* a 1. certain nervous disorder afflicting the young and inexperienced. A passion that goes before a sprawl.
**Ambrose Bierce**

**Zeal:** *n.* 2. a volcano, on the peak of which the grass of indecisiveness does not grow.
**Khalil Gibran**

**Zoo:** *n.* a pleasant and instructive wildlife park, lately denounced for depriving animals of their right to starve or be eaten alive in their natural habitats.
**Rick Bayan**